35 Strategies for Guiding Readers through Informational Texts

TEACHING PRACTICES THAT WORK

Diane Lapp and Douglas Fisher, Series Editors

Designed specifically for busy teachers who value evidence-based instructional practices, books in this series offer ready-to-implement strategies and tools to promote student engagement, improve teaching and learning across the curriculum, and support the academic growth of all students in our increasingly diverse schools. Written by expert authors with extensive experience in "real-time" classrooms, each concise and accessible volume provides useful explanations and examples to guide instruction, as well as step-by-step methods and reproducible materials, all in a convenient large-size format for ease of photocopying.

35 Strategies for Guiding Readers through Informational Texts
Barbara Moss and Virginia S. Loh

The Effective Teacher's Guide, Second Edition:
50 Ways to Engage Students and Promote Interactive Learning
Nancy Frey

Dare to Differentiate, Third Edition:
Vocabulary Strategies for All Students
Danny Brassell

35 Strategies for Guiding Readers through Informational Texts

Barbara Moss and Virginia S. Loh

Series Editors' Note
by Diane Lapp and Douglas Fisher

THE GUILFORD PRESS
New York   London

© 2010 The Guilford Press
A Division of Guilford Publications, Inc.
72 Spring Street, New York, NY 10012
www.guilford.com

Printed in the United States of America

This book is printed on acid-free paper.

Last digit is print number: 9   8   7   6   5   4   3   2   1

Library of Congress Cataloging-in-Publication Data

Moss, Barbara, 1950–
    35 strategies for guiding readers through informational texts / Barbara Moss,
and Virginia S. Loh.
        p.   cm. — (Teaching practices that work)
    Includes bibliographical references and index.
    ISBN 978-1-60623-926-1 (pbk. : alk. paper)
    1. Language arts.   2. Thought and thinking—Study and teaching.
3. Literacy.   I. Loh, Virginia Shin-Mui. II. Title. III. Title: Thirty-five
strategies for guiding readers through informational texts.
    LB1576.M8216 2010
    428.4071—dc22
                                                            2010022240

About the Authors

Barbara Moss, PhD, is Professor of Literacy Education in the Department of Teacher Education at San Diego State University. She has taught English and language arts in elementary, middle, and high school settings, and has worked as a reading supervisor. In addition to her role as a university professor, she presently works as a literacy coach at an urban high school in San Diego. Dr. Moss's research focuses on issues surrounding the teaching of informational texts at the elementary and secondary levels. She regularly presents at professional conferences at the local, state, national, and international levels, and has published numerous journal articles, columns, book chapters, and books. She is coeditor (with Diane Lapp) of two other books recently published by The Guilford Press: *Teaching New Literacies in Grades K–3: Resources for 21st-Century Classrooms* and *Teaching New Literacies in Grades 4–6: Resources for 21st-Century Classrooms*.

Virginia S. Loh, EdD, is a part-time faculty member at San Diego State University, Director and Educational Consultant for Wells Academics, Ghosteditor/Entrepreneur of In the Margins, and a former K–8 schoolteacher. Her doctoral dissertation, for which she received a Beiter Research Grant Award from the Children's Literature Association, was a qualitative study on the cultural authenticity of Asian American children's literature. She has published peer-reviewed articles and conducted presentations on this topic. Dr. Loh has worked with diverse student populations and has a strong knowledge of instructional methods, assessments, and educational research and theories. She has her Multiple Subject and Cross-Cultural Language and Academic Development teaching credentials. Dr. Loh is committed to teacher excellence, educational policymaking, and student achievement, and she is actively involved in community boards and organizations. She is coauthor (with Carolyn Marsden) of the children's book *The Jade Dragon*.

Series Editors' Note

As our schools continue to grow in linguistic, cultural, and socioeconomic diversity, educators are committed to implementing instruction that supports both individual and collective growth within their classrooms. In tandem with teacher commitment, schools recognize the need to support teacher collaboration on issues related to implementing, evaluating, and expanding instruction to ensure that all students will graduate from high school with the skills needed to succeed in the workforce. Through our work with teachers across the country, we've become aware of the need for books that can be used to support professional collaboration by grade level and subject area. With these teachers' questions in mind, we decided that a series of books was needed that modeled "real-time" teaching and learning within classroom instruction. Thus the series *Teaching Practices That Work* was born.

Books in this series are distinguished by offering instructional examples that have been studied and refined within authentic classroom settings. Each book is written by one or more educators who are well connected to everyday classroom instruction. Because the series editors are themselves classroom teachers as well as professors, each instructional suggestion has been closely scrutinized for its validity.

35 Strategies for Guiding Readers through Informational Texts, by Barbara Moss and Virginia S. Loh, contains lesson examples that support learning to read, write, and converse about nonfiction topics that span the curriculum areas. As educators realize, most students become very proficient at reading narratives because they are able to make interesting connections between their lives and the story plots. Utilizing these connections, the authors draw on the reader appeal of texts in the Information Age to create teacher-friendly lessons designed to expand vocabulary, comprehension, and writing for students in grades K–12. Lessons support students' contrastive analysis of topics by inviting them to develop a critical literacy perspective.

To support additional topical investigations, the authors also include lists of related leveled texts and magazines.

We invite you into the "real-time" teaching offered in this book and hope you'll find this series useful as you validate and expand your teaching repertoire. And if you have an idea for a book, please contact us!

DIANE LAPP
DOUGLAS FISHER

Introduction

Increasingly, teachers across the country have discovered the value of using authentic literature in order to supplement textbooks and basal readers; such literature is usually found in the form of trade books. Teachers use these books in the classroom for a variety of purposes, including but not limited to guided reading, shared reading, independent reading, and/or content-area instruction. Most of the time, however, teachers employ fiction (or stories) rather than informational texts. Fictional stories are certainly important; the narrative structures are familiar to students and offer access to content-area information in a narrative format. Furthermore, such texts provide hours of reading pleasure to adults and children alike.

Times are changing, however. Today's students are living in an age of information, globalization, and digitalization. They are constantly bombarded with and surrounded by information from a variety of sources beyond books and magazines. These texts have one important thing in common: their purpose is to inform the reader. These sources include the World Wide Web, television/cable, radio/podcasts, social networking sites, texting, e-mail, and many more. Information can literally be accessed from the palms of our hands through cell phones that are equipped to send and receive information. Today's students are at the forefront of advancing communication technologies. So, what does this all mean for classroom teachers?

The need for today's teachers to involve students, even primary graders, in reading expository or non-narrative-type text is more important than ever before. As students move through the grades, the amount of expository reading required increases significantly. By high school, 90% of the material students read is expository or informational text. As adults, too, most of what we read at work and at home is expository text. If students are to survive in the workplace in the Information Age, they must be able to read the language of information: exposition. The ability to gain information from the Internet, for example, is dependent on the ability to read and understand exposition. Much of the material found on standardized tests is expository in nature. If students are going to succeed on these tests, they need exposure to and understanding of how expository text works. If students are to become responsible citizens and future leaders, they must be taught how to think about and use the information they receive. Simply being able to locate information is not enough. Whether in school or in the workplace, it is imperative that students be able to evaluate the truth value of the information they access. For these reasons, we would like to make a case for using critical literacy as a framework for learning through informational texts.

Because students are inundated with information, they may have difficulty differentiating between what's important versus interesting, what's "true" and what's "really true," and so on. Information can be biased and, as a result, students need the ability to critically examine data to determine their truth value. Teaching students how to read and comprehend critically will empower them to make better and more informed decisions and opinions, which is the ultimate goal of teaching informational texts. Critical literacy encourages us to examine how people and ideas are represented and to investigate embedded and/or implicit messages (Morgan, 1997). Boutte (2002) contends that even young children can be taught to be critical readers, to "learn to identify and clarify ideological perspectives in books" (p. 147). Many of our biases may have been the result of the accumulation of both subtle and overt messages in books, media, and instructional practices (Boutte, 2002); thus, learning how to recognize issues of power and perspective by assuming a critical perspective is necessary. In short, teachers would be remiss to not push students to critically and constructively think about, categorize, and label all the information they are receiving.

Contrary to popular belief, however, learning through informational text is not just a bitter pill that students must swallow in order to succeed in school. Studies indicate that many students actually *prefer* reading informational text to fiction. With the incredible array of enticing informational resources available today, it is easier than ever to engage students in real-world reading. Regardless of a student's area of interest, whether video games, hip-hop, rocks, horses, tattoos, dinosaurs, medieval weaponry, outer space, or art, informational texts can fuel this curiosity and deepen comprehension and understanding. These are the materials that answer our questions about the universe—about the people, places, and things students encounter in their daily lives. Too often, though, we don't capitalize on our students' fascination with facts. Instead, we fill our classrooms with stories—fantasies and realistic tales—ignoring the excitement for reading that information might ignite.

This newly revised and expanded edition of *25 Strategies for Guiding Readers through Informational Texts* (Moss, 2003) is designed to provide classroom teachers in grades K–12 with a practical resource for introducing the uses of informational text in the classroom. Like the earlier volume, this book is intended to help teachers guide students in learning about strategies for understanding these texts. It differs from the previous edition in several ways, however. First of all, we have added 10 new strategies, bringing the total to 35 strategies. In many instances, these are examples of newer strategies than those included in the original book. In addition, we have tried to create a better balance between strategies appropriate for students across the grade levels. For example, we have added several additional strategies appropriate to primary-grade students, as well as more that can be used in grades 7–12. In addition to these changes, we have updated the examples and increased the emphasis on critical literacy and the importance of using a wide variety of text types.

The strategies in the book are organized according to the following topics: Getting Started, Building Background, Vocabulary, Comprehension, and Writing. A shaded box beneath each strategy indicates the topic it addresses. Each strategy is also identified by its recommended grade levels.

A common format is used to explore each strategy. Each strategy is explained and described in the "What Is It?" section. A rationale for using each strategy is provided in the "What Is Its Purpose?" section, and specific, step-by-step procedures for using the strategy are described in the "What Do I Do?" section. The "Example" section describes how the strategy might be implemented in a classroom with students at a specific grade level, and a list of references gives teachers more information on the strategy. The final section, "Your Turn!", provides directions for using the reproducible forms and templates, designed for student use.

At the end of the book is an appendix of recommended materials, including trade books categorized according to level. In the strategies, primary books are coded P and are intended for grades 1–3; intermediate-level books are coded I and are intended for grades 4–6; middle-level books are coded M and are intended for grades 7–9; and books coded YA (young adult) are suitable for use with high school students. The appendix also includes a listing of informational magazines for children and young adults, as well as a brief list of useful informational websites.

Most of the strategies included in this book are suitable for use with the many wonderful student magazines available today, including *Time for Kids, Kids Discover, Sports Illustrated Kids, Cobblestone,* and many others. Most of the strategies can be used with newspaper articles, websites, or any other sources of informational text. The strategies included in this book can also be used to teach textbook information in virtually every content area, including science, social studies, and mathematics.

We would like to acknowledge Drs. Diane Lapp and Douglas Fisher for their help in developing this project. We hope that you will enjoy using *35 Strategies for Guiding Students through Informational Texts* and that it will be a useful resource as you begin to involve your students in developing their understanding of informational text. We hope, too, that your students will develop an increased enthusiasm for informational text that will prompt them to find pleasure and enjoyment in this type of reading.

BARBARA MOSS
VIRGINIA S. LOH

References

Boutte, G. S. (2002). The critical literacy process: Guidelines for examining books. *Childhood Education, 78*(3), 147–152.

Morgan, W. (1997). *Critical literacy in the classroom: The art of the possible.* New York: Routledge.

Moss, B. (2003). *25 strategies for guiding readers through informational texts.* San Diego, CA: Academic Professional Development.

Contents

PART FOUR

Comprehension Strategies

PART FIVE

Writing Strategies

PART ONE

Getting
Started
Strategies

Strategy 1

Selecting Informational Texts

GRADE LEVELS: K–12

Getting Started
Building Background
Vocabulary
Comprehension
Writing

What Is It?

Choosing informational texts is different from selecting fictional texts. Informational texts contain factual information and include trade books, e-books, websites, newspapers, magazines, and so on. They don't usually have characters or plots, so selecting these materials on the basis of compelling characters or fast-paced plots does not work. Whether choosing materials for a whole class or for individual reading, teachers need to apply different criteria to the selection of informational texts. Teachers should use what they know about their students' interests and abilities to select materials that will be appealing to their students. Not only should materials be picked on the basis of their relevance to classroom topics of study, but also on the basis of their overall quality.

What Is Its Purpose?

The purpose of carefully selecting informational texts is to provide students with rich experiences in reading quality materials that can inform or educate. Through such experiences students can develop knowledge, gain exposure to non-narrative text structures, reinforce content learning, and learn to evaluate information for its "truth value," a critical skill in the 21st century. By teaching students to evaluate the quality of a text on their own, we provide them with critical literacy skills. By asking students to consider the five A's listed below, we help to ensure that they don't just accept information from a text, but reflect on its meaning and point of view.

What Do I Do?

When evaluating informational materials, teachers should consider the five A's (adapted from Moss, 2002):

1 The AUTHORITY of the author:

- Who is the author of the book or article or publisher of the website?

- What are the author's or publisher's qualifications for writing the book or article or creating the website?

2 The ACCURACY of the text content:

- Are the text and visual matter accurate?

- Does the author explain where he or she got his or her information?

- Does the author cite experts or provide references or a bibliography that validates the information?

- Does the book or website explore more than one side of an issue or does it represent only one point of view? Does it appear to be biased? Is the information current?

3 The APPROPRIATENESS of the text for the age group of the audience:

- Is the level of difficulty and writing style appropriate to the audience?

- Are there headings and subheadings that help the reader move through the text?

- If it is a website, does it load quickly? Is it easy to navigate?

- Do the pictures and visuals support the text?

4 The literary ARTISTRY:

- Does the material read like an encyclopedia entry or is it written in an engaging style?

- Does the author use a "hook" to get readers interested in the material?

- Does the author use metaphors, similes, and other literary devices to help readers better understand the information?

5 Kid APPEAL:

- ◆ Does the text include interesting visuals?

- ◆ Is the text one that appeals to students at your grade level?

- ◆ Would you pick up the book or go to the website on your own?

Please note ...

The titles listed in the appendix at the end of this book are trade books, magazines, and websites that meet the criteria listed above. Trade books of high quality are also listed on the website of the National Council of Teachers of English's (NCTE) Orbis Pictus Award for Outstanding Nonfiction for Children (*www.ncte.org/awards/orbispictus*). This award is given annually by the NCTE for the most outstanding nonfiction book for children. Another important award for informational books is the Robert F. Sibert Informational Book Medal (*www.ala.org/ala/mgrps/divs/alsc/awardsgrants/bookmedia/sibertmedal/*), given annually by the American Library Association to the most outstanding informational book of the year. Another great resource for locating quality informational texts, both books and websites, is *Book Links* (*www.ala.org/BookLinks*), a publication of the American Library Association. This resource features bibliographies of fiction and informational titles for children and young adults arranged according to themes. It also indicates whether books are available in paperback.

Example

Eighth-grade American history teacher James Hernandez decided to begin involving his students in selecting and reading more informational texts during sustained silent-reading time. He introduced his students to the five A's described above and used this book to model for students how to evaluate the quality and "truth value" of an informational text. To facilitate the development of these critical literacy skills, James modeled how to complete the informational text Evaluation Form using the website *www.martinlutherking.org*, a racist website that advocates the abolition of Martin Luther King Day. He demonstrated for students how to identify the publisher of the site, how to evaluate the accuracy of the information, and how to recognize the bias of the site's creator. He then explained to students that they needed to locate at least one book or website related to their next unit of study, the Civil Rights Movement. They would then evaluate this book or website. James consulted the school librarian to help him identify some potential titles related to this topic. After students identified their texts, they completed the Informational Text Evaluation Form and shared their findings in small groups.

References

Book Links. Retrieved from *www.ala.org/booklinks*.

Martin Luther King, Jr.: A true historical examination. Retrieved from *www.martinlutherking.org*.

Moss, B. (2002). *Exploring the literature of fact*. New York: Guilford Press.

Orbis Pictus Award for Outstanding Nonfiction for Children. Retrieved from *www.ncte.org/awards/orbispictus*.

Robert F. Sibert Informational Book Medal. Retrieved from *www.ala.org/ala/mgrps/divs/alsc/awardsgrants/bookmedia/sibertmedal*.

Your Turn!

Locate an informational text suitable for your grade level either in the appendix at the back of this book, or one of your own choosing. Use the rating sheet on the next page to evaluate the text you have chosen.

Informational Text Evaluation Form

Title of Text _____

Part 1: Authority of the Author	YES	NO
Is the author or website publisher identified?		
Does the author or publisher have expertise in the topic?		
Part 2: Accuracy	**YES**	**NO**
Are the text and pictures accurate?		
Are there references or a bibliography that validates the information?		
Does the book or website explore more than one side of an issue or does it represent only one point of view?		
Does it appear to be biased?		
Is the information current?		
Part 3: Appropriateness	**YES**	**NO**
Is the level of difficulty and writing style appropriate to the audience?		
Is the book or website well organized and easy to navigate?		
Do the pictures and visuals support the text?		
Are there headings to aid the reader?		
Part 4: Literary Artistry	**YES**	**NO**
Did the author use a "hook" to get you into the text?		
Did the author use literary devices to keep you interested?		
Part 5: Kid Appeal	**YES**	**NO**
Does the text have interesting visuals?		
Would you pick up the book or go to the website on your own?		

········· **Strategy 2** ·············

Informational Text Interest Survey

GRADE LEVELS: K–12

Getting Started
Building Background
Vocabulary
Comprehension
Writing

What Is It?

An Informational Text Interest Survey is a way for teachers to learn about students' interests related to topics typically found in informational books, magazines, or newspapers. Most interest surveys focus on students' interests related to stories. Informational Text Interest Surveys, conversely, help teachers identify things about the real world that may be of interest to students, such as hobbies, famous people, interesting places, animals, and so on.

What Is Its Purpose?

The information gained from an Informational Text Interest Survey can help teachers make selections about classroom book read-alouds, as well as match readers with books, magazine or newspaper articles, websites, and so forth, on topics of passionate personal interest like surfing, music, art, or ancient civilizations. This compelling interest may result in silent, independent reading, which may lead to improved reading achievement and/or an increase in students' schema for a topic. Surveys can also provide teachers with information that can help them in selecting informational text read-alouds as well as other informational book choices. However, Informational Text Interest Surveys should not be used in isolation. They should be complemented with teacher observations, student interviews, and other informal ways of identifying student interest. Noting students' fictional reading preferences, for example, may give teachers ideas for informational texts they would enjoy.

What Do I Do?

1 In order to assess students' informational text reading interests, teachers can use interest surveys like the one shown on the next page as a starting point. First, look over the sentence stems provided.

2 Decide which stems are most suitable for the ages and abilities of your students or create your own questions. With younger students or struggling readers and writers, you may want to conduct interviews rather than asking students to write out their answers.

3 Have students complete the survey or interview. Compile a master list indicating which students have interests in common. This list can be useful for creating interest groups or for involving groups of students in reading texts about topics on which they share an interest.

4 Begin to match students with texts that meet their interests. These can include informational trade books, newspaper and magazine articles, or websites. The California Department of Education online lists of recommended literature (*www.cde.ca.gov/ci/rl/ll*) can be useful for locating books on a particular topic. They allow you to type in the name of a topic and generate a list of related informational books. Other resources for locating informational texts are listed in the appendix.

Example

Teacher Karen Carter teaches sixth-grade struggling readers in San Diego, California. She has many students who are English language learners. The majority of her students find reading and writing difficult. Karen asked her strong readers and writers to complete the stems on the Informational Text Interest Survey on the next page. Karen chose to conduct interviews based on several of the stems on the survey with those students unable to complete the survey in writing. After giving students the survey, Karen analyzed their responses to the stems and the choice items at the end. She found, for example, that a number of students were interested in soccer. She decided to locate as many books and magazine articles on soccer as she could in order to use their interest as a springboard for motivating them to read. She also located websites on soccer and bookmarked them for student use. In addition, she found that her students expressed an interest in topics like World War II, art, music, and jungle animals. Karen consulted a variety of resources and found books and other print and nonprint resources related to these topics that would be appropriate for her students. These resources included recent book reviews as well as the California Department of Education website mentioned earlier. In this way, she was able to match her students with materials of interest to them.

References

California Department of Education Recommended Literature for Mathematics and Science. Retrieved from *www.cde.ca.gov/ci/sc/ll/index.asp*.

California Department of Education Recommended Readings in Literature K–12. Retrieved from *www.cde.ca.gov/ci/rl/ll*.

National Council for the Social Studies Notable Trade Books for Young People. Retrieved from *www.ncss.org/resources/notable*.

Your Turn!

Try out the Informational Text Interest Survey with your class. You may need to adapt the questions to the ages and abilities of your students. Then, use the findings from this survey to match readers with books.

Informational Text Interest Survey

Directions: Please write the answer to each statement on the line provided.

1 I'd like to learn about _____

and _____ during this year.

2 One famous person I'd like to read about is _____.

3 Magazines I like to read include _____

_____.

4 One sport I'd like to read about is _____.

5 One science topic I'm interested in is _____.

6 One social studies topic I'm interested in is _____.

7 My favorite hobby is _____.

8 My favorite subject in school is _____.

9 An informational text I've read before and liked was _____

_____.

10 When I'm not in school, I like to _____

_____.

11 When I use the Internet, I like to read about _____

_____.

12 Put an "X" next to the topics you would like to read about:

Animals	Dinosaurs	Experiments
Oceans	Space	Famous people
Birds	Music	Art
Cooking	Dance	History
Crafts	Sports	Pets

Reading Informational Texts Aloud

GRADE LEVELS: K–12

Getting Started
Building Background
Vocabulary
Comprehension
Writing

What Is It?

Informational text read-alouds provide students with opportunities to listen to non-story-type texts. They present teachers with the opportunity to help students access informational texts; in this way, teachers can introduce a unit of study or support student understanding of content that may be beyond the students' reading level.

What Is Its Purpose?

These texts expand students' knowledge, teaching them concepts and terms related to a variety of topics and people. They sensitize students to the patterns of exposition, which are far less familiar to students than stories. They spark interest in a topic, enrich literature study, and provide tie-ins to many curricular areas. Most important of all, they can ignite student interest in a variety of topics, leading to silent, independent reading. This silent reading is a critical factor in the development of lifelong readers.

Informational text read-alouds can introduce, culminate, or provide new information about a cross-curricular unit. For example, when beginning a unit on the

Civil Rights movement, a teacher might read *MLK: Journey of a King* (Bolden, 2008).

What Do I Do?

Informational text read-alouds can take one of several formats:

1 Read "bits and pieces." Bits-and-pieces read-alouds include single chapters of book sections of a given title. They can involve the reading of short magazine or newspaper articles, or sections of longer articles. Excerpts from collective biographies like *Lives of the Artists: Masterpieces, Messes (and What the Neighbors Thought)* (Krull, 1995), *Lives of the Musicians: Good Times, Bad Times (and What the Neighbors Thought)* (Krull, 2002), *Lives of the Athletes: Thrills, spills (and What the Neighbors Thought)* (Krull, 1997), or *Lives of Extraordinary Women: Rulers, Rebels (and What the Neighbors Thought)* (Krull, 2000), for example, make excellent 5-minute read-alouds. These breezy thumbnail sketches of the lives of prominent artists, musicians, athletes, and women teach today's students about outstanding achievers from the past and the present.

2 Read picture captions. Reading picture captions can whet student appetites for information. Captions from *Anne Frank: Beyond the Diary* (Van der Rol & Verhoeven, 1993) connect artifacts back to the diary itself. Reading captions from titles like) *Mission: Planet Earth: Our World and Its Climate—and How Humans Are Changing Them* (Ride & O'Shaughnessy, 2009) or *Surprising Sharks!* (Davies, 2008) create motivation for reading prompted by the engaging visuals provided by both of these titles.

3 Break up the reading. If the text is complex or full of unfamiliar concepts, you may want to read the text over a period of days. Even informational picture books on complicated content-related topics may fall into this category. Identify logical breaking points, and read a short section of text at one sitting rather than the entire work.

4 Link informational texts with other genres. For example, linking uniquely interactive titles like *Letters for Freedom: The American Revolution* (Rife, 2009) with poetry like *Colonial Voices: Hear Them Speak* (Winters, 2008) helps teachers build students' schema about this important period in history.

5 Read different books about the same person or topic. For example, reading three different biographies of Johnny Appleseed, Amelia Earhart, or Martin Luther King, Jr. can illustrate to students the different points of view an author can take about a person or topic. These types of reading experiences help students develop a critical stance toward what they are reading; they teach them that different sources of information may contradict one another and that different authors can take different perspectives on the same person.

6 Plan before, during, and after reading activities. Because informational text is often more difficult for students to understand than fiction, it is even more important that they engage in before, during, and after reading experiences with this type of text. It is particularly important that students participate in meaningful prereading experiences, since they may have little prior knowledge about the topics addressed in these works.

Before Reading

Establish links between students' experiences and text materials. Use Anticipation Guides (Strategy 5), KWHL (Strategy 6), or Table of Contents Prediction (Strategy 8) to engage students in the topic. Bring in props, pictures, or examples of things mentioned in the story to make information more concrete to students. For example, pictures of the incredible gold artifacts found aboard the Spanish galleon ship *Atocha* can enhance children's enjoyment of Gail Gibbons's (1990) *Sunken Treasure*. Before students read, help them to notice text features like bold headings, text boxes, the table of contents, and the index. By pointing out headings and the table of contents, teachers can help students understand the cues the author provides to the text organization. In this way, students will find it easier to comprehend the information.

During Reading

Answer questions, clarify terms, and guide students in completing graphic organizers like Data Charts (Strategy 21), Venn Diagrams (Strategy 25), or Semantic Maps (Strategy 23). Through such activities, teachers can help focus student attention on making meaning from the text.

After Reading

Involve students in creative extensions to the text. Activities like completing Discussion Webs (Strategy 20), participating in Readers' Theatre (Strategy 30), and writing Two-Column Journals (Strategy 31) provide meaningful extensions to children's reading experiences.

Example

Teacher Lorena Cortez reads informational texts aloud to her fourth graders on a regular basis. She selects read-alouds that link to content-area topics like science and social studies and often uses these books to introduce or expand upon textbook content. She sometimes reads aloud a small section from a larger text, such as when she read aloud the profile of Van Gogh from *Lives of the Artists: Masterpieces, Messes and What the Neighbors Thought)* (Krull, 1995) to introduce an art lesson. On other occasions, she reads aloud books that she knows will be of interest to her students and that have the potential to motivate them to read on their own.

When planning read-alouds for her students, Lorena creates before, during, and after reading experiences that maintain student engagement. The Informational Book Read-Aloud Planning Guide included with this lesson provides guidelines for planning these experiences. Before reading *The Book of Stars* (Twist, 2007), Lorena provided students with an Anticipation Guide (Strategy 5) designed to help her evaluate students' prior knowledge about stars. Lorena previewed the text with her students, noting the unique format of the book that included pages of different sizes, bold titles such as *The Sun, Red Dwarf, Giant Star,* and more; she also previewed the placement, types, and topics of the text boxes. She pointed out to students that the book was organized topically, with each section focused on a different type or aspect of stars.

Because the text contained dense information, Lorena chose to read only one section per day. As she read, she helped students create a Data Chart (Strategy 21) that allowed them to compare information about different stars, including their diameters, their temperatures, distances from earth, myths and legends, and so on. After reading, students compared the information in their science text with that found in the trade book. This furthered their ability to compare and critically analyze information.

References

Bolden, C. (2008). *MLK: Journey of a king*. New York: M. Abrams. (P).

Davies, N. (2008). *Surprising sharks!* New York: Candlewick. (P).

Gibbons, G. (1990). *Sunken treasure*. New York: HarperCollins. (I).

Krull, K. (1995). *Lives of the artists: Masterpieces, messes (and what the neighbors thought)*. San Diego, CA: Harcourt Brace. (YA).

Krull, K. (1997). *Lives of the athletes: Thrills, spills (and what the neighbors thought)*. San Diego, CA: Harcourt Brace. (YA).

Krull, K. (2000). *Lives of extraordinary women: Rulers, rebels (and what the neighbors thought*. San Diego, CA: Harcourt Brace. (YA).

Krull, K. (2002). *Lives of the musicians: Good times, bad times (and what the neighbors thought)*. San Diego, CA: Sandpiper. (M, YA)

Ride, S., & O'Shaughnessy, T. (2009). *Mission: Planet earth: Our world and its climate—and how humans are changing them*. New York: FlashPoint. (M, YA).

Rife, D. (2009). *Letters for freedom: The American revolution*. New York: Kids Innovative. (I).

Twist, C. (2007). *The book of stars*. New York: Scholastic. (I).

Van der Rol, R. & Verhoeven, R. (1993). *Anne Frank, beyond the diary: A photographic remembrance*. New York: Viking. (M)

Winters, K. (2008). *Colonial voices: Hear them speak*. New York: Dutton. (I).

Your Turn!

Select an informational text to use as a read-aloud either from the appendix at the back of this book, or one of your own choosing. Before you choose, however, consider what format you will use to read the book aloud. Record that information on the form on the next page. In addition, record notes about what you will do before, during, and after the reading.

Informational Book Read-Aloud Planning Guide

1 What informational text do you plan to read aloud? _____

_____

2 What format do you plan to use for this read-aloud? _____

_____

_____

3 What will you do before, during, and after reading this book?

	Strategies
Before Reading:	
How will you activate prior knowledge about the topic? What new words will you need to introduce? How will you teach students about the text organization (review headings, table of contents, etc.)	Anticipation Guide KWHL Chart Table of Contents Prediction? Other: _____
During Reading:	
How will you help students understand the readings?	Point out headings Review table of contents Point out signal words Other: _____
After Reading:	

How will students demonstrate what they have learned?	Ask/answer questions
	 Complete a graphic organizer
	    Venn Diagram
	    Data Chart
	    Cause–Effect Map
	    Problem–Solution Outline
	
	 Other: _____
	 Draw a picture
	 Complete a quickwrite or Two-Column Journal
	 Do a project
	 Think–pair–share what students have learned
	
	 Other: _____

············· **Strategy 4** ·······················

Shared Reading
with Informational Texts
and Text Feature Search

GRADE LEVELS: K–12

Getting Started
Building Background
Vocabulary
Comprehension
Writing

What Is It?

The shared-reading strategy teaches students how expository text works and how it differs from narrative text. Shared reading is a strategy that scaffolds student reading of books they may not be ready to read themselves. It can be particularly useful as a way to introduce the unique characteristics of informational texts. The Text Feature Search engages students in looking for and exploring those text features they have learned about during shared reading.

What Is Its Purpose?

Shared Reading with Informational Texts helps teachers demonstrate how this type of text works and how it differs from narratives. Demonstrations and discussions of the features found in these two types of texts can develop students' metacognitive awareness of the characteristics of the two text types and adds to prior knowledge about the nature and purposes of informational texts. Once teachers have shared these features with students through shared reading, they can use the Informational Text Feature Search form to locate and reflect on the purposes of those features.

What Do I Do?

Shared reading can be done with big books for younger students or with textbooks or trade books for older students. To do a shared reading, the teacher should:

1 Set up an enlarged informational book on an easel, distribute multiple copies of an informational trade book or article, or project the text using an overhead or document camera. This allows everyone to see the text in order to follow along.

2 Involve students in making predictions about the text using the following questions as a guide:

- What kind of book/text is this?
- How do you know?
- What kind of information do you expect to find?
- What kind of illustrations do you expect to find?
- What do you know about the author?
- Who is the publisher and/or funding source?

3 Focus student attention on the various features of expository text, using the following questions as a guide:

- What do the headings and subheadings tell me?
- What parts of the book help me find information?
- How is the information organized?
- How do I read the diagrams (or maps, graphs, timelines)?

4 Next, demonstrate and explain how students can use locational devices like tables of content, indices, glossaries, and headings to help them locate specific information:

- What is the table of contents for? When and how is it used?
- What are the page numbers for?
- Why are the pages numbered?
- What is the index for? When and how is it used?
- Do all information books have contents and indices? Why? Why not?

5 Point out visual information including charts, graphs, maps, diagrams, and timelines. Use the following questions as a guide:

◆ Why do authors include visual information in maps, graphs, or timelines?

◆ How are these maps, graphs, and timelines the same? How are they different?

◆ How is reading a "visual text" different from reading a regular text?

6 Point out to students that we never depend on one data source. We need to research topics using several sources in order to make an informed opinion about the topic. Point out the need to consider the accuracy and validity of the content. Use the following questions as a guide:

◆ Where did the author get his or her information?

◆ What sources are listed in the bibliography or references?

◆ What do you know about the topic? Is there anything that you want to explore or need more information about?

7 At this point, teachers should bring in fiction and informational texts for comparison purposes. Focus on the differences between the two types of texts using the following questions as a guide:

◆ Do we read informational books the same way as stories? Why? Why not?

◆ What are some of the differences in the way we read the two text types?

◆ What do informational books have that stories do not?

◆ What do storybooks have that informational books do not?

◆ Why are the two text types different? (Moss, 2002).

Example

Teacher Evelyn Craig used shared reading to introduce her third graders to the similarities and differences between fiction and informational texts using two simple texts, *Frog and Toad Are Friends* (Lobel, 1979) and *Toad or Frog?* (Stewart & Salem, 2003). Using these two texts, she demonstrated for her students the differences between the two using the questions listed above. She previewed an informational enlarged text, involving students in making predictions about the text. After that, she introduced students to the access features of expository text, like tables of contents, indices, and glossaries, by pointing them out in the enlarged text. She also pointed out visual information, including charts, graphs, maps, diagrams, and timelines. Following this, Evelyn allowed teams of students to select their own informational trade books. She involved students in completing an Informational Text Feature "scavenger hunt" by locating pages numbers where each feature was found and recording the purpose of each feature on the line provided (an example is provided below).

Sample Informational Text Feature Search

Book Title _Poison Dart Frogs_

Author _Tracy Reeder_

Feature	✓	Page #	Purpose
Table of contents	✓	3	To tell where chapters are
Headings	✓	6, 8, 9, 10, 11	To tell you what is in that section
Bolded words	✓	9, 10, 11	To show you the new words
Glossary	✓	31	To define the new words
Index	✓	32	To help you look up topics
Sidebars		none	
Fact box	✓	12, 13, 14	To give small bits of information
Captions	✓	22, 24	To tell what the picture is about
Photographs	✓	almost every page	To help you understand the information
Diagrams		11	To show a poison dart frog's life cycle
Tables		none	
Graphs		none	
Maps	✓	7	Shows where grasslands are
Flowcharts		19	Show how a frog sheds its skin
Webs		none	
Timelines		none	
Maps		23	Shows where to find poison dart frogs are found

References

Lobel, A. (1979). _Frog and Toad are friends_. New York: Harper Collins. (P).

Moss, B. (2002). _Exploring the literature of fact_. New York: Guilford Press.

Stewart. J., & Salem, L. (2003). _Toad or frog?_ New York: Continental Press. (P).

Your Turn!

Plan a shared-reading experience like the one described above. Focus students on identifying the features of informational texts and comparing those features with the characteristics of fictional texts. Once you have completed this activity, provide students with an informational trade book and have them complete the Informational Text Feature Search provided on the next page. Have them locate each of the features and list the page number on which they found the feature. In addition, have students write down the purpose of each feature in the last column. The teacher will need to model for students how to complete this task by completing the first few items with the students.

Informational Text Feature Search

Directions: Check the features that you found in your text. You may add additional features at the bottom of the list. List the page number for the page you found it on, and write its purpose.

Book Title _____ **Author** _____

Feature	✓	Page #	Purpose
Table of contents			
Headings			
Bolded words			
Glossary			
Index			
Sidebars			
Fact box			
Captions			
Photographs			
Diagrams			
Tables			
Graphs			
Maps			
Flowcharts			
Webs			
Timelines			
Maps			
References			

Building Background
Strategies

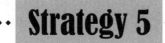

Strategy 5

Anticipation Guide

GRADE LEVELS: K–12

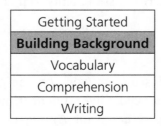

Getting Started
Building Background
Vocabulary
Comprehension
Writing

What Is It?

Anticipation Guides (called *prediction guides* by Herber, 1978) are a prereading strategy that can be used with informational texts such as newspaper articles or textbooks at a variety of levels. Before they read, students respond to carefully worded statements that focus their attention on the topic to be learned.

What Is Its Purpose?

Anticipation Guides help students activate their prior knowledge and arouse their curiosity about the topic at hand. Students then read to confirm or disconfirm their reactions to the statements presented before they read. After they read, they have the opportunity to go back and change their responses based upon what they have learned from their reading.

Anticipation Guides can be used with any content, but are especially useful with science-related content. Many students have misconceptions about science-related information. Anticipation Guides can help students confront and later reflect upon their misconceptions. Anticipation Guides can also be used with material from any content area, including English, social studies, health, or mathematics.

What Do I Do?

Anticipation Guides require preparation on the part of the teacher. Here are suggested steps in creating and using Anticipation Guides:

1 Analyze the text to identify key ideas and information.

2 Anticipate ideas from the text that help students reflect on what they know about the topic and are interesting, controversial, or thought provoking.

3 Create four to seven written statements that students will label true or false.

4 Develop directions for the activity.

5 Before they read have students work on the guide in pairs or teams after the topic has been briefly introduced. Give students time to discuss their responses to the statements as a large group. When using Anticipation Guides with younger students, teachers often read the items aloud and let them do "thumbs up/thumbs down" as a group response to each statement.

6 After reading, give students the opportunity to change their answers based on their new information. Review the guide with the whole class, asking students to identify how they have changed their responses based on their new information.

Example

High school history teacher Dale Newton wanted to prepare his students for the study of the Industrial Revolution as part of a 10th-grade history class. Prior to reading the chapter in the textbook, Dale had his students work in pairs to complete the following Anticipation Guide designed to activate their prior knowledge and arouse their curiosity about the topic. Before reading the book chapter, students were required to answer "T" to the statements they thought were true and "F" to those they thought were not true. After completing the guide in pairs, students shared their responses with the whole group. After students completed their reading of the textbook chapter, Dale asked them to review their guides and work with their partners to change their answers based on what they had learned. He then led the group in a discussion of their answers and how they had changed them.

After reading, students changed their answers to reflect their new information. They then discussed these changes as a large group.

Sample Anticipation Guide

T   F   1. Industrialization is always good for workers because it creates jobs.

T   F   2. It could be argued that the potato crop contributed to industrialization in England.

T   F   3. England could not have industrialized without its many rivers.

T   F   4. Large numbers of cities sprang up well before the Industrial Revolution.

T   F   5. Entrepreneurs had the capital needed to invest in machines.

T   F   6. Early industrialization helped make the United States the powerful country it is today.

T   F   7. Inventions like the steam engine and cotton gin improve life for everyone in a society.

T   F   8. Economic cooperation is better than competition in a society.

References

Herber, H. (1978). Prediction as motivation and an aid to comprehension. In H. Herber, *Teaching reading in content areas* (2nd ed., pp. 173–189). Englewood Cliffs, NJ: Prentice-Hall.

Your Turn!

Select a text from the appendix at the end of this book or one of your own choosing. Create an Anticipation Guide for your students using the form on the next page. Have students work in pairs to complete it. Give students the chance to change their answers after they read the text.

Anticipation Guide for _____

_____

Directions: Circle "T" for the statements you agree with, and "F" for the ones you disagree with. After you have read the material, go back and change your answers based on your new information.

T   F   **1.** _____

T   F   **2.** _____

T   F   **3.** _____

T   F   **4.** _____

T   F   **5.** _____

T   F   **6.** _____

T   F   **7.** _____

T   F   **8.** _____

T   F   **9.** _____

T   F   **10.** _____

······· **Strategy 6** ·······

KWHL

GRADE LEVELS: K–12

Getting Started
Building Background
Vocabulary
Comprehension
Writing

What Is It?

KWHL (Ogle, 1992) is an adaptation of the KWL strategy (Ogle, 1986). It helps students activate their prior knowledge about a topic and strategically locate information as they read. During the first step of KWHL students identify what they *know* (K) about a topic. They brainstorm a list of things they know related to the topic and record these in the first column of a chart. During the second step, students identify what they *want to know* (W) about the topic. They pose questions and record these questions in the second column of a chart. These questions later provide a purpose for their reading. For the third step, students list *how* (H) they could answer the questions. For example, students could mention using their textbooks, reference materials (dictionaries, Internet research, class charts, etc.), research methodologies (research, survey, etc.), and/or specific text features as ways to answer the questions. After reading, students have the opportunity to identify what they have *learned* (L) about the topic. They record the answers to their questions in the third column of the KWHL Chart.

What Is Its Purpose?

KWHL Charts are designed to arouse curiosity about a text, activate prior knowledge, and engage students in identification of their own questions about a topic as well as available information sources. They also provide a record of what students have learned through their reading.

What Do I Do?

1 Select a book, newspaper, or magazine article appropriate to your students' abilities.

2 Prepare copies of a KWHL Worksheet or create a KWHL Chart on large chart paper or a transparency. The worksheet or chart should be divided into four columns, with the "K" column on the far left, the "W" and "H" columns in the middle, and the "L" column on the right.

3 Activate students' prior knowledge about the topic of the text by asking them to brainstorm what they know about the topic. Have them record this information under the "K," or "What I Know," column.

4 Involve students in generating questions they want to answer as they read. Have them record these questions under the "W," or "What I Want to Know," column of the chart.

5 Have students list ways they can answer the questions in the "H," or "How I Will Find Out," column.

6 Involve students in reading or listening to you read a text aloud. Instruct them to read or listen to find the answers to the questions they posed. Then have them record their answers to the questions in the "L," or "What I Learned," column.

Example

Second-grade teacher Maria Gomez created a KWHL lesson for the book *Ant Cities* (Dorros, 1987) prior to beginning a unit on insects. She created a large KWHL Chart on a piece of chart paper. Before she read the book aloud to her students, she asked them to work in pairs to brainstorm what they already know about ants. She recorded each team's response in the far left "K," or "What I Know," column of the chart. Students then teamed once again to discuss what they *want to know*. Maria listed these questions in the middle column or "W" ("What I Want to Know") portion of the chart. At this point, Maria asked the students to think about how they might locate the answers to their questions, and she recorded these responses in the

"H" ("How I Will Find Out") column. She then read the book aloud, directing the children to listen for the answers to the questions they posed. After listening to the reading, students worked in pairs once again to brainstorm answers to the questions posed earlier. Maria then completed the "L," or *What I Learned*, column of the chart (see example below).

Sample KWHL Chart for _Ant Cities_

K (What I Know)	W (What I Want to Know)	H (How I Will Find Out)	L (What I Learned)
Ants build hills	What do ants eat?	Internet research Textbook	Insects plants sweets termites
Ants are red	Where do ants live?	Online encyclopedia Textbook	In a nest with lots of rooms
Ants like to eat sweets	Can ants smell?	Internet research	Yes, they smell with their antennas

References

Dorros, A. (1987). *Ant cities*. New York: Crowell. (P).

Ogle, D. (1986). K-W-L: A teaching model that develops active reading of expository text. *Reading Teacher, 39*, 563–570.

Ogle, D. (1992). KWL in action: Secondary teachers find applications that work. In E. K. Dishner, T. W. Bean, J. E. Readence, & D. W. Moore (Eds.), *Reading in the content areas: Improving classroom instruction* (3rd ed., pp. 270–282). Dubuque, IA: Kendall Hunt.

Your Turn!

Select a text from the suggested list in the appendix, one of your own choosing, or a magazine or newspaper article. Involve your students in completing the KWHL Chart on the next page by identifying the "K," "W," and "H" columns before they read and the "L" column after they read.

KWHL Chart for _____

K (What I Know)	W (What I Want to Know)	H (How I Will Find Out)	L (What I Learned)

I See … I Wonder … I Know …

GRADE LEVELS: K–6

Getting Started
Building Background
Vocabulary
Comprehension
Writing

What Is It?

I See … I Wonder … I Know … (adapted from Oczkus, 2004) is a strategy designed to help students to activate prior knowledge and develop curiosity about the topic of a text by using the illustrations and headings as stimuli for their thinking. Before reading, students write or draw what they see in the illustrations and/or headings ("I See … ") and record questions that reflect what they wonder about what they see ("I Wonder … "). After reading the text they record in the "I Know … " column the answers to the questions posed in the "I Wonder … " column. They can also record additional things that they learned from the text.

What Is Its Purpose?

Understanding text features like illustrations and headings are essential to understanding informational texts. The purpose of this strategy is to focus student attention on the illustrations and headings found in informational texts. This strategy can focus attention on the importance of carefully reading and attending to illustrations and headings. Furthermore, it prompts student to not only identify illustrations and headings, but to pose questions about the content and locate answers to those questions as they read. In this way it provides a purpose for their reading.

What Do I Do?

1 Select a single informational text, whether a textbook or a trade book. As an alternative, each student can read a different informational text.

2 Get students to predict what the text will be about through a brief examination of the cover, title, and illustrations.

3 Using short "chunks" of text, model for students how to think about what they see in the illustrations and headings. Demonstrate for them how to record what they see in the "I See … " column of the chart in words or pictures. In addition, the teacher needs to model for students how to complete the sentence starter "I wonder … " with a question they have about the illustration or heading. The teacher can next read a section and model how to complete the "I Know … " column.

4 Give students guided practice in using this strategy by projecting illustrations and headings from a text on the document camera. Take students through the completion of the chart, letting them work with a partner to complete each of the first two columns. Then read a small section of text and have them complete the third column. At this point students should be able to use the strategy independently.

Example

Third-grade teacher Belinda Sanchez's students were studying biomes. They had addressed this topic with the help of their textbook, but Belinda wanted to extend their learning. She located an excellent website on the topic on Thinkquest.com (*library.thinkquest.org/08aug/00473/spotlight.htm*). She wanted to involve her students in reading the information on the website, but she knew that they would need her support in order to do this successfully. She decided to focus on three different biomes for the first lesson: grasslands, rain forests, and deserts. To focus student attention on the illustrations and headings found on the website, she decided to use the I See … , I Wonder … , I Know … strategy.

Belinda began the lesson by showing students the radio buttons for each of the three types of biomes. She clicked on the button for the first biome, grasslands, and pointed out the headings that appeared on the page, which included Climate, Animals That Live in Grasslands, and What Are Grasslands? She also pointed out the photograph of grasslands on the web page. At this point she thought aloud and modeled for students how to complete the "I See … " and "I Wonder … " portions of the chart. Belinda noted that the word *grasslands* appeared on the first page several times and in each of the headings. She then showed students how to complete the "I See … " column of the chart (see chart below). She then modeled for students how to create an "I Wonder … "statement based on the "I See … " column. She recorded "I wonder what grasslands are" in that column and created two additional "I Wonder … " statements based on the headings and the photograph.

Sample I See … I Wonder … I Know … Chart

I See …	I Wonder …	I Know …
I see *the words grasslands in the first heading.*	I wonder *what grasslands are.*	I know *that grasslands contain grasses.*
I see *that one heading is about animals that live in the grasslands.*	I wonder *what animals live in the grasslands and why they live there.*	I know *that rabbits, ducks, buffalo, cheetahs, and lions live in grasslands.*
I see *in the photograph that the grasslands are very green.*	I wonder *how they get water for the grasslands.*	I know *that grasslands get water from rain.*

After Belinda modeled the "I Wonder … " statements she read the information about the grasslands aloud, asking students to listen to see whether they could answer the "I Wonder … " questions. At this point she asked students to locate the answers in the text. She helped students record their responses in the "I Know … " column. At this point, she asked students to follow the same steps with the sections on the rain forest and deserts. Students worked in pairs to complete their charts.

References

Oczkus, L. (2004). *Super six comprehension strategies: 35 lessons and more for reading success.* Norwood, MA: Christopher Gordon.

Biomes ThinkQuest. Retrieved from *library.thinkquest.org/08aug/00473/spotlight.htm.*

Your Turn!

Select an informational text from the list in the appendix at the back of this book or one of your own choosing. Model for your students how to complete the I See … , I Wonder … , and I Know … chart. Then have them complete the "I See … " and "I Wonder … " columns before they read the text and the "I Know … " column afterward.

I See . . . , I Wonder . . . , I Know . . . Chart

Directions: Preview the headings and illustrations in your book. Record the page number in column 1, what you see in column 2, and what you wonder about what you see in column 3. After you have read the text, record the answers to your "I Wonder . . . " questions in the "I Know . . ." column.

Page	I See . . .	I Wonder . . .	I Know . . .
	I see	I wonder	I know
	I see	I wonder	I know
	I see	I wonder	I know

Strategy 8

Table of Contents Prediction

GRADE LEVELS: K–12

Getting Started
Building Background
Vocabulary
Comprehension
Writing

What Is It?

Table of Contents Prediction is a strategy uniquely suited to informational texts. It can be used at all grade levels. Table of Contents Prediction involves having students make predictions about informational text content by creating a table of contents for the text based on their predictions. By reading the title and examining the cover of a book, students can begin to think about the content found within its covers. In addition to identifying possible topics within the text, creating a table of contents for the text requires students to consider how the text might be organized.

What Is Its Purpose?

The purpose of Table of Contents Prediction is to help students activate their prior knowledge about a topic and make predictions about possible text content. This strategy forces students to speculate about the topics that will be addressed in an informational text. It also engages students in the examination of text organization, since they must not only identify content, but consider how it is organized in the table of contents.

What Do I Do?

1 Have students locate a table of contents in a text. Review with students what a table of contents is and how it helps the reader understand the topic to be studied, the organization of the information provided in the text, and how it helps the reader locate information.

2 Provide students with a variety of informational trade book titles that have a table of contents or give them the title of a textbook chapter or Internet site.

3 Instruct students to not open the books. Ask them to consider the title and examine the cover of the book if available.

4 Pair students with a partner. Provide them with the Table of Contents Prediction handout.

5 Ask students what they think the table of contents might include. Instruct them to also think about how the information in the table of contents will be organized. Have them record their table of contents on the handout.

6 Ask students to share the table of contents they have created with the whole class.

7 Have students open their books to compare their table of contents with the one the author used. Emphasize that there is no one way to organize information; the author could use many different ways.

Example

Marilyn Cates teaches second graders who are learning about informational texts. While her students have developed skill in making predictions about narrative texts, she is interested in helping them learn to predict content found in informational texts.

Marilyn began the Table of Contents Prediction lesson by reviewing with students the form and purposes of a table of contents. She had students turn to the table of contents in their social studies text. She showed them the titles of each section of the table of contents and its page number and location. She helped her students see that the title of the section in the table of contents matched the chapter title found on the page indicated. Marilyn used the book *The Life Cycle of an Earthworm* (Kalman, 2004) to demonstrate that the table of contents indicates how the text is organized. Students could clearly see that the text is arranged chronologically.

After this introduction, Marilyn handed out a number of easy-to-read informational trade books from the National Geographic Society that contained tables of contents. She instructed students to not open the books. She modeled for students how to examine the cover and title, and then she created a sample table of contents for one of the books on the Table of Contents Prediction handout. She then had the whole group create a table of contents for a different book.

At this point Marilyn arranged students in pairs and let each pair select a book. The students created a table of contents for their texts and recorded them on the form (see below). Marilyn next invited students to share their books and tables of contents with the class. One pair of students' table of contents is shown below for the book *Time for Kids: Our World* (Walsh, n.d.).

Sample Table of Contents Prediction

Title of Book ___Our World___   Author ___Kenneth Walsh___

Chapter 1 ___Water and Our World___

Chapter 2 ___Air and Our World___

Chapter 3 ___Plants and Our World___

Chapter 4 ___Deserts and Our World___

Finally, Marilyn told students to open their books and look at the table of contents. Students discussed with their peers the ways in which their table of contents were similar to or different from the one in the text. Marilyn reminded students that authors arrange information in many different ways, and that there is no one way to organize information in an informational text.

References

Kalman, B. (2004). *The life cycle of an earthworm*. New York: Crabtree. (I).
Walsh, K. (n.d.). *Time for kids: Our world*. New York: Time. (I).

Your Turn!

Introduce your students to Table of Contents Prediction using a textbook or trade book from the list in the appendix in the back of this book or one of your own choosing. Have them complete the Table of Contents Prediction form provided on the next page.

Table of Contents Prediction

Directions: Look over the front and back covers of your book without opening it. What do you think the titles of the chapters will be? What order will they be in? Record your answers below.

Title of Book _____ **Author** _____

Write your predictions for the chapters in this book on the lines below.

Chapter 1 _____

Chapter 2 _____

Chapter 3 _____

Chapter 4 _____

Chapter 5 _____

Chapter 6 _____

You may add more chapters below if needed.

•••••••••••••••••••••••••• **Strategy 9** ••••••••••••••••••••••••••

Imagine, Elaborate, Predict, and Confirm

GRADE LEVELS: 4–12

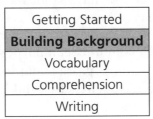

| Getting Started |
| **Building Background** |
| Vocabulary |
| Comprehension |
| Writing |

What Is It?

The Imagine, Elaborate, Predict, and Confirm (IEPC) strategy (Vacca & Vacca, 2008) requires students to visualize (Imagine) and verbalize (Elaborate), which is an important skill for reading comprehension. In addition, the IEPC strategy encourages students to make predictions (Predict) and to refer to text to check or to modify these predictions (Confirm). In this way, students are also working on their critical thinking skills. This strategy is especially helpful for supplementing texts that are not supported by pictures. (As students enter the upper grades, more and more of their readings are text intensive.)

The IEPC strategy also works as an anticipatory activity in that students are introduced to a topic, apply their prior knowledge, and then asked to learn more about the topic.

What Is Its Purpose?

According to Lenihan (2003), many students, particularly English language learners and struggling readers, have difficulty creating mental images of a text, especially if the text is a chapter book or a book without pictorial support; as a result, these students also have a difficult time comprehending the content. The IPEC strategy encourages students to use visual imagery and prediction skills in order to enhance their text comprehension.

What Do I Do?

The procedures for the IEPC strategy are as follows (Wood, 2001):

1 Select a text that is related to the topic of study. Then, select a specific passage that contains content appropriate for developing imagery and that introduces the topic to be studied.

2 Distribute the IEPC chart or have students fold a piece of paper horizontally into four columns labeled accordingly.

3 Point out the "Imagine" column: Set a purpose for reading and tell the students to imagine a scene as you read the passage out loud. Have students close their eyes and encourage them to use their senses by thinking about the tastes, smells, sights, and feelings associated with the topic.

4 Ask students to record their images in either words or pictures in the "Imagine" column. If they draw their images, ask students to label them as well.

5 Have students share their images with a partner or with a group.

6 Point out the "Elaborate" column: Have students consider the initial responses of their classmates. Ask them to think of additional details associated with the scene they originally visualized. The following questions can be used to prompt their responses:

- What did you learn from talking to your classmates?
- What had you forgotten that you remembered when talking to your classmates?
- What textual connections can you make? (For example, have the students make a text-to-self, text-to-text, or text-to-world connection.)

7 Ask students to record their elaborations in the "Elaborate" column.

8 Point out the "Predict" column: Have students use the information they wrote in the previous two columns to make predictions about the content found in the rest of the text. Ask the following guiding questions:

- What do you think the rest of the book will be about?
- What do you think will happen next?

9 Ask students to record their predictions in the "Predict" column.

10 Have students read the rest of the text independently or read the text aloud to the class.

11 Point out the "Confirm" column: During and after reading, encourage students to refer to their predictions. Ask the following questions:

- ◆ Were you able to confirm your predictions? Cite evidence from the text.
- ◆ Did you have to modify your predictions based on what you learned from the text? If so, how and why?

12 Ask students to record their confirmations and modifications in the "Confirm" column.

Example

Mrs. Franny Prall teaches 12th-grade U.S. Government. During the last couple weeks of school, she wanted to address the topic of social activism. As her students were heading off to college, she wanted them to feel a sense of political and personal agency. She had them study contemporary personas who have made a significant difference in shaping national policies such as Barack Obama, the first African American president of the United States; Aung Sang Suu Kyi, the figurehead for Burma's struggle for democracy; Vaclav Havel, the first president of the Czech Republic; and Nelson Mandela, the South African civil rights leader.

In addition to these famous world leaders, Mrs. Prall also wanted to demonstrate how an "average" person could make a difference. For this reason, she chose to introduce her students to Greg Mortenson, an American mountain climber turned humanitarian who builds schools in Central Asia. As her text, she used *Three Cups of Tea: One Man's Journey to Change the World … One Child at a Time* (Thomson, Mortenson, & Relin, 2009). This version is adapted for young adults; it is shorter and more child centered than the original bestseller.

Mrs. Prall distributed an IEPC Chart and read an excerpt from the book describing how Greg Mortenson's daughter felt about her father being away all the time to build schools for children in disenfranchised countries and how she dealt with the perils he faced that included death threats. Mrs. Prall set the purpose for reading by telling students that she wanted them to pay attention to how global tensions can impact individual families. She asked her students to visualize and imagine how the little girl must have felt. Then, she had them discuss their imaginings and record their elaborations in the "I" and "E" columns of the chart, respectively. Next, she asked students to predict what they thought the rest of the book would be about. For homework, she had them read various sections of the book. In class the next day, they completed the "Confirm" (C) section of the chart. She followed up with a whole-class discussion.

The IEPC strategy served as a springboard for a writing task Mrs. Prall assigned in which she asked students to write about how they are personally affected by global tensions such as the war in Iraq, the economic downturn, global warming, and so on, and what they can do about them, globally and locally.

References

Lenihan, G. (2003). Reading with adolescents: Constructing meaning together. *Journal of Adolescent and Adult Literacy, 47*(1), 8–12.

Thomson, S., Mortenson, G., & Relin, D. O. (2009). *Three cups of tea: One man's journey to change the world … one child at a time.* New York: Puffin. (YA).

Vacca, R. T., & Vacca, J. L. (2007). *Content area reading: Literacy and learning across the curriculum* (9th ed.). Boston: Allyn & Bacon.

Wood, K. D. (2001). *Literacy strategies across the subject areas: Process-oriented blackline masters for the K–12 classroom.* Boston: Allyn & Bacon.

Your Turn!

Select an informational trade book addressing a topic relevant to your curriculum. Use a text from the appendix at the back of this book or a text of your own choosing. Carefully identify a text with a good introductory passage that will evoke imagery and anticipation. (It would be helpful for the students to use a text about which they have some prior knowledge of the topic.) Instruct students to close their eyes and to record their mental images under the "I" column on the IEPC Chart. Then, model how to elicit elaborations (E) and predictions (P). And lastly, show them how to refer to the text to confirm and/or modify (C) their thinking.

IEPC Chart

IMAGINE I	ELABORATE E	PREDICT P	CONFIRM C

PART THREE

Vocabulary
Strategies

Word Map

GRADE LEVELS: 2–12

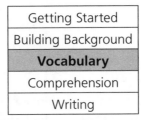

| Getting Started |
| Building Background |
| **Vocabulary** |
| Comprehension |
| Writing |

What Is It?

Word Maps (Schwartz & Raphael, 1985) provide a way for students to organize conceptual information as they seek to not only identify, but also understand, a word. This particular map illustrates the class or category to which the concept belongs, the attributes or characteristics of the concept, and examples of the concept. Word Maps can be used for students in grades 3 and up, and are equally effective as a pre- or postreading activity.

What Is Its Purpose?

Word Maps are useful for introducing students to vocabulary they are likely to encounter while reading or for helping them to reflect on word meanings after they have completed their reading. They engage students in thinking deeply about words and give them the opportunity to record their thoughts on a visual organizer. In this way, students increase their understanding of the academic vocabulary found in various content areas.

What Do I Do?

1 To create a Word Map, the teacher or students first write the name of the concept being addressed in the center of the map.

2 They then answer the question "What is it?" by thinking of a word or phrase that best indicates the answer to this question.

3 After that, students need to identify and list three examples of the concept ("What are some examples?") in the appropriate boxes.

4 Then, students identify attributes or properties of the concept ("What is it like?"). More advanced students might be encouraged to list metaphors and similes for the word.

Example

Third-grade teacher Alan Brugman's students were studying civil rights during African American History month. They studied the life and work of Martin Luther King Jr., Rosa Parks, and other civil rights leaders. As part of that study, Alan read the book *Teammates* (Golenbock, 1992) aloud to his class. *Teammates* is the story of the friendship between Jackie Robinson, the first black man to play major league baseball, and his teammate, Pee Wee Reese, a white man from the South.

Prior to reading, Alan presented his students with the Word Map focusing on the word *discrimination* (see example below). He explained the term to his students and distributed copies of the Word Map to each child. He helped the students fill in the box containing the question "What is it?" with the answer "prejudice" or "being mean to others who are different in some way" after explaining the term to the students. He asked them to think about the word *discrimination* as he read the book aloud. After he read the book, he asked students to think of other words that tell what discrimination is like. Students gave the answers "mean," "unfair," and "making fun" as examples. Finally, he asked the students to work with a partner to list three examples of discrimination as described in the book. An example of their completed Word Map is found below:

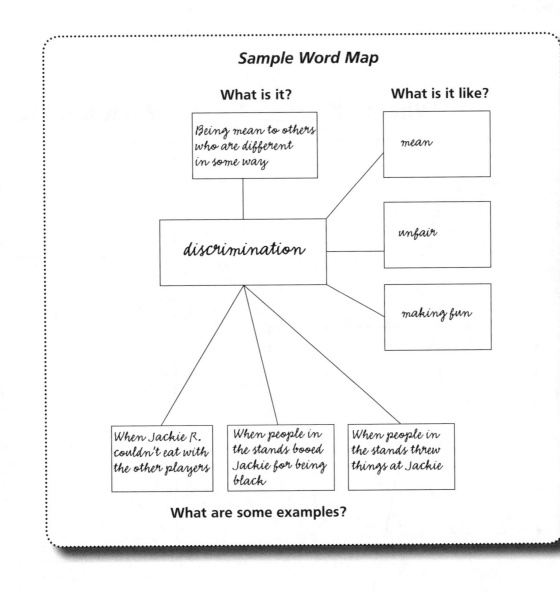

Sample Word Map

What is it?   **What is it like?**

Being mean to others who are different in some way

discrimination

mean

unfair

making fun

When Jackie R. couldn't eat with the other players

When people in the stands booed Jackie for being black

When people in the stands threw things at Jackie

What are some examples?

References

Golenbock, P. (1992). *Teammates*. San Diego, CA: Harcourt Brace Jovanovich. (I).

Schwartz, R. M., & Raphael, T. (1985). Concept of definition: A key to improving students' vocabulary. *The Reading Teacher, 39,* 198–205.

Your Turn!

Select a text from the appendix at the back of this book or one of your own choosing. Write a word for a critical concept found in the book in the middle of the Word Map. Before and/or after students read the text, have them fill in the boxes on the Word Map, answering the questions "What is it?" "What is it like?" and "What are some examples?"

Word Map

Directions: Put the word you are studying in the box in the middle. Then complete each of the other boxes.

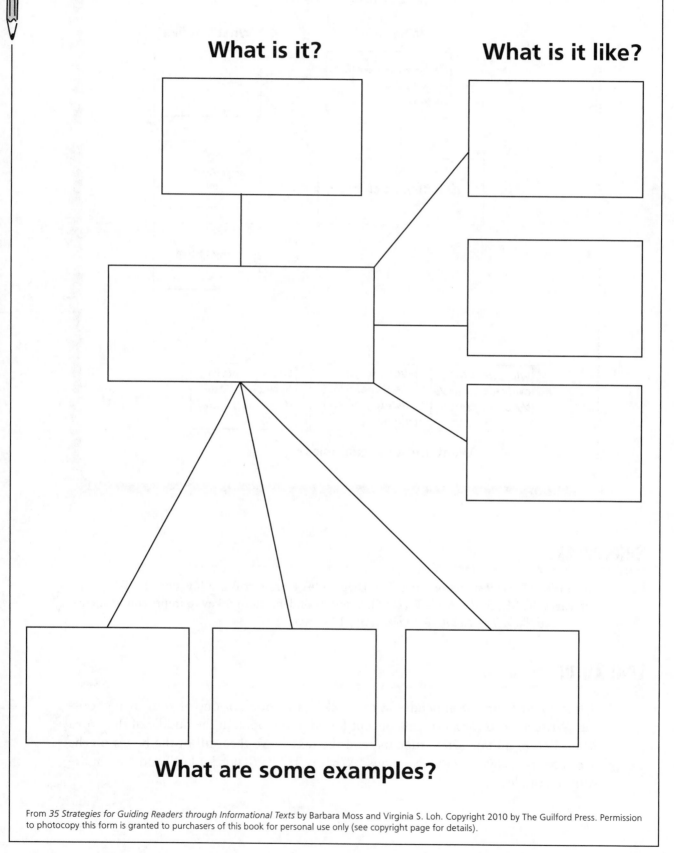

What is it?

What is it like?

What are some examples?

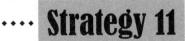

Strategy 11

List–Group–Label

GRADE LEVELS: 2–12

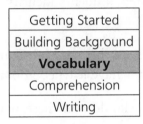

Getting Started
Building Background
Vocabulary
Comprehension
Writing

What Is It?

List–Group–Label (Taba, 1967) is a form of brainstorming that helps students make predictions about the vocabulary they will encounter in a particular content area. This strategy can be used with informational trade books, magazine articles, or textbook content. This strategy goes beyond basic brainstorming since students do not simply predict possible vocabulary they will encounter, but they also categorize those terms. List–Group–Label is useful for students of almost all ages and can involve them before, during, and after reading.

What Is Its Purpose?

The purpose of List–Group–Label is to help students see relationships among words. It requires students to move beyond memorization of definitions to categorization of related words. By categorizing and then labeling groups of words, students develop greater awareness of the connections between words and concepts.

What Do I Do?

1 Select an appropriate informational text. Trade books or textbooks work best for this activity.

2 Before they read, ask students to *list* words they know related to the topic addressed in the reading material. They can complete this step individually, in pairs, or in small groups. These words should be recorded on a worksheet (see example).

3 Ask students to *group* or cluster related words into categories. These word groupings should be recorded on the worksheet.

4 After completing this step, students identify words that can serve as *labels* for each category.

5 At this point, students read the material. During their reading, students should jot down new words that they have learned about the topic.

6 After reading, students should add these new terms to those identified before their reading, placing them in the appropriate category. They may wish to record these words on their worksheet using different color ink from the words they generated before reading.

Example

Mary Chaney, a sixth-grade history teacher, used the book *Tales Mummies Tell* (Lauber, 2003) to introduce a unit on Ancient Egypt. In order to activate students' prior knowledge before reading the book, she asked students to brainstorm a list of words related to the topic of mummies. The students' list appears below:

> Found in Egypt
> Buried in big tombs
> Buried thousands of years ago
> Wrapped in cloth
> Certain organs were removed
> Preserved over time
> Usually kings and queens
> Put in wood coffins
> Buried with food and jewels

After they listed these ideas, students grouped them into categories. They then labeled the categories. Their categories and labels are listed below:

Where mummies were buried	Who they were	How mummies were buried	When mummies were buried
Found in Egypt	Usually kings and queens	Wrapped in cloth	Buried thousands of years ago
Buried in big tombs		Put in wood coffins	
		Buried with food and jewels	
		Certain organs were removed	
		preserved over time	

Following their reading, students added more information to each category and also chose to add a new category entitled "Why scientists study them" (see p. 58) The **bolded** words indicate ideas that were added to the original categories.

References

Lauber, P. (2003). *Tales mummies tell*. New York: Scholastic. (M).

Taba, H. (1967). *Teacher's handbook to elementary social studies*. Reading, MA: Addison-Wesley.

Your Turn!

Select a text from the appendix at the back of this book or one of your own choosing. Involve your students in completing the List–Group–Label strategy. Students should begin by brainstorming what they know about the topic. Then they can group and label their words by categories. Students can record their answers on the worksheet included on the next page.

Sample List–Group–Label

Where mummies were buried	Who they were	How mummies were buried	When mummies were buried	Why scientists study them
Found in Egypt	Usually kings and queens	Wrapped in cloth	Buried thousands of years ago	To learn where diseases come from
Buried in big tombs	Can be animals	Put in wood coffins	As long ago as 2,100 years	To learn how diseases have changed
Found in South America, Italy, United States, Russia, and China	Included cats and crocodiles	Buried with food and jewels		To learn how long people lived
	In ancient Peru, everyone was mummified	Certain organs were removed		To learn what people ate
		Preserved over time		
		Buried with their possessions		
		Mummification ended with Christianity		

List–Group–Label

Directions: Before you read, **LIST** 10 words related to the topic of your book.

1

2

3

4

5

6

7

8

9

10

Now, **GROUP** all the words that have something in common in one column. Then make up a name for the category. This is a **LABEL**. Write it in the square at the top of the column. Then do the same for each of the remaining columns.

After you read the book, add new words that you have learned to each column.

Word Sort

GRADE LEVELS: 2–12

Getting Started
Building Background
Vocabulary
Comprehension
Writing

What Is It?

Word Sorts (Gillet & Kita, 1979) are a way to help students understand the content-related vocabulary found in a text. Word Sorts help students discover relationships among words and categorize words based on those relationships. Word Sorts differ from List–Group–Label (Strategy 11). With List–Group–Label, students themselves generate words related to a topic. With Word Sorts, teachers identify the key words about a topic in advance and involve students in arranging them logically. There are two types of Word Sorts—open sorts and closed sorts. Open sorts require students to determine their own categories for like words that have been grouped together. No two students will generate exactly the same categories in an open Word Sort. With closed sorts, the teacher provides students with the categories ahead of time and the students sort the words with these categories in mind. Closed sorts are typically easier for students because the categories have been provided for them. Word Sorts can be used as a prereading activity to activate students' prior knowledge about the vocabulary in a text. They can also be used as a postreading activity to assess student understanding of what has been read.

What Is Its Purpose?

Like List–Group–Label, the purpose of a Word Sort is to help students see relationships between words found in informational texts. By sorting words that the teacher has identified, students gain familiarity with the new vocabulary in the text.

What Do I Do?

1 Select a content-related text. Identify 15–20 critical terms related to the topic at hand.

2 Select terms that have relationships to one another so that they can be categorized. Write the words on 3" × 5" cards or print them on the computer on business card-size printer forms. Create enough sets of cards so that each pair of students will have a set. If you are doing a closed sort, write the category names in all capital letters on the appropriate number of cards.

3 Introduce the Word Sort activity before or after students read.

4 Give each pair of students a set of cards. Read the words to the students, asking them about the meanings of words that are new to them. Be sure that the words are arranged in alphabetical order or scrambled (not in categories) when you give them to the students.

5 If students are completing a closed sort, list the categories they will be using on the board. If students are doing an open sort, tell them to group words that have relationships to one another and label those words with a category name card.

6 Circulate around the room to check on students' progress. Then ask students to explain how they categorized the words and why.

Example

Seventh-grade science teacher Carol Newman was teaching a unit on endangered species. To make this issue more relevant to her San Diego, California, students, she decided to use Caroline Arnold's (1993) *On the Brink of Extinction: The California Condor*. This book describes how the efforts of the San Diego Zoo led to the reintroduction of the California condor into the wild after its near extinction. This book could serve as an introduction to the students' visit to the San Diego Zoo, where they would have the opportunity to see the condors and learn about scientists' efforts to save them.

Carol introduced the book by engaging students in a discussion of what they already know about endangered species. She then assigned students to read the book and discuss it in small groups over the next 2 weeks. After students completed their reading, she had them form pairs to complete this open Word Sort. She explained the Word Sort strategy, and gave each pair of students a set of word cards.

vultures	boxes	6 oz.	DDT	shooting
cliffs	caves	57 days	15,000'	urbanization
crop	scavengers	mice	poison	social
pip	10' wingspan	primaries	55 mph	monogamous

Students then sorted their words into groups and identified the category terms at the top of each column.

Characteristics	Breeding areas	Causes of extinction	Flight	Chicks
vultures	caves	DDT	55 mph	57 days
10' wingspan	cliffs	poison	15,000'	pip
social	boxes	shooting	primaries	6 oz.
scavengers		urbanization		crop
monogamous				mice

After completing the sort, students explained and compared their word clusters and provided rationales for the categories they developed.

References

Arnold, C. (1993). *On the brink of extinction: The California condor.* New York: Harcourt Brace Jovanovich. (I, M)

Gillet, J., & Kita, M. (1979). Words, kids and categories. *The Reading Teacher, 32,* 538–542.

Your Turn!

Select a text from the appendix at the back of this book or one of your own choosing. Create a list of words related to the book that can easily be categorized. Have students list these terms on the sheet on the next page. If you prefer, you may put the words on cards. Then, pair students and have them sort the words and identify categories for each cluster. Have students discuss their sorts and provide a rationale for the way they grouped the words.

Word Sort

1   **Directions:** List the words to be sorted here.

_____   _____   _____

_____   _____   _____

_____   _____   _____

_____   _____   _____

2   Cluster similar words. List related words on the lines. Write the category name in the top box of each column.

Concept Circles

GRADE LEVELS: K–12

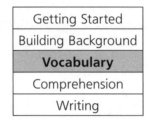

Getting Started
Building Background
Vocabulary
Comprehension
Writing

What Is It?

A Concept Circle (Vacca & Vacca, 1999) is a way for students to study words and relate those words to one another. Concepts Circles are circles that have been divided into sections. Words and/or phrases can be put in each section of the circle. Students examine the words in each section of the circle and name or describe the concept relationship among the sections.

Concept Circles are a most versatile strategy and are useful with students of all ages. Teachers can use Concept Circles to have students identify characters in a story, to identify geographical concepts like plateau, tundra, or steppe, or to identify scientific terms like *photosynthesis* or *mitosis*. They are a motivating strategy that can be modified in ways that make them more challenging. Furthermore, Concept Circles are an easy strategy for students to create on their own.

What Is Its Purpose?

Concept Circles help students develop the ability to generalize based on specific information. They provide a motivating, engaging way for students to understand content-area concepts.

What Do I Do?

1 To create Concept Circles, the teacher simply identifies key concepts he or she wants students to learn.

2 The teacher creates circles and divides them into as many key sections as are needed.

3 Next, the teacher should put words related to the target concept into each section (see example below).

4 Finally, the teacher draws a line under the circle where students will record the concept word.

Modifications of this strategy can involve including a word or phrase that does not belong in one section of the circle or leaving some circle sections blank so that the students can complete them. These activities require that students identify characteristics that do not belong to a particular concept and produce examples of features that do belong.

Example

Fourth-grade teacher Zoë Allen was involving her students in a study of the human body as part of a science unit. Her students had recently completed their reading of textbook content on this topic, as well as listening to portions of *iOpeners: All about the Body* (Sinclair, 2006). In order to review the characteristics of each body system, she asked her students to complete the following Concept Circles. The stu-

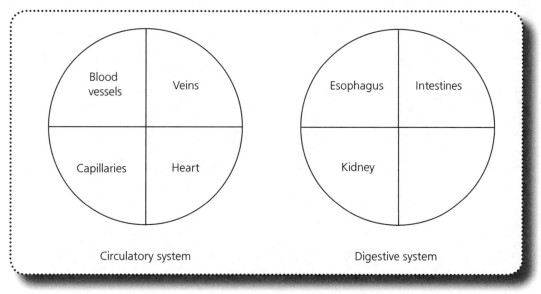

dents used the clues within each circle to determine the system being described. On one circle, Zoë left one section of the circle blank for the students to complete.

References

Sinclair, J. (2005). *iOpeners: All about the body.* New York: Pearson. (I).
Vacca, R., & Vacca, J. (1999). *Content area reading.* New York: HarperCollins

Your Turn!

Select a text from the list in the appendix at the end of this book, or one of your own choosing. Model for your students how to complete a Concept Circle that addresses the main concepts in the book. Then have them create and complete the other Concept Circles on the following page. As your students become more proficient, they can create their own Concept Circles.

Concept Circles

Directions: Look at the words in each section of the circle. Think of a word that those words describe and write it on the line below the circle.

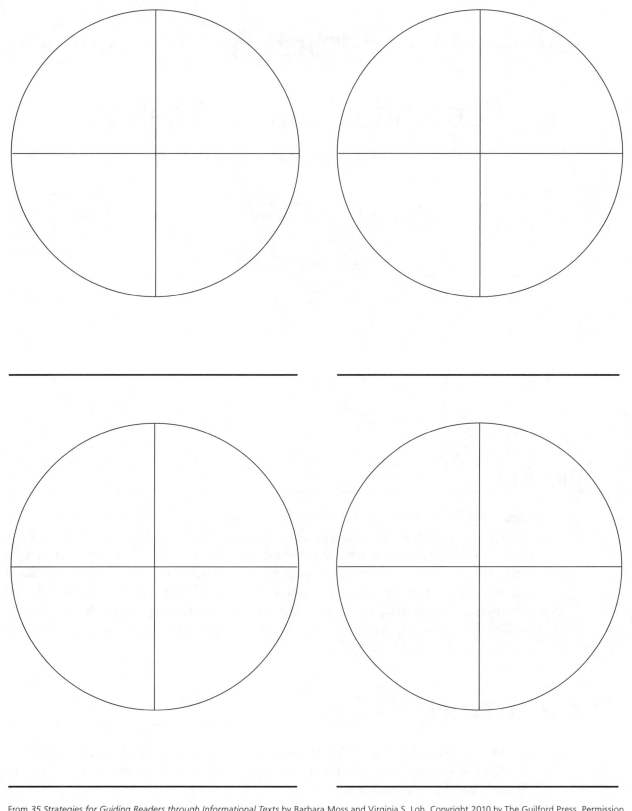

Strategy 14

Semantic Feature Analysis

GRADE LEVELS: 3–12

Getting Started
Building Background
Vocabulary
Comprehension
Writing

What Is It?

Semantic Feature Analysis (Anders & Bos, 1986) is an activity where students identify important features or characteristics of a concept on a matrix and analyze similarities and differences among those concepts. Semantic Feature Analysis can be used as a prereading activity to activate what students know about words. Students can then reexamine their matrix after reading to clarify and amend their initial responses on the matrix. It can also be used as a postreading comprehension check to determine whether students understand how particular concepts are alike and different.

What Is Its Purpose?

Semantic Feature Analysis helps students visually compare and contrast concepts through the use of a matrix. It helps students to draw conclusions based upon the information that is represented.

What Do I Do?

1 The teacher must first identify a category of concepts in the topic being taught. For example, the category might be transportation.

2 The teacher must then identify several terms within the category. Using the example of transportation, the teacher might identify terms like *bicycle* or *car*. Then he or she would identify features they share, such as tires or seats.

3 The terms are listed in the left-hand column and the shared features are listed across the top (see example for snakes below).

4 Students then identify whether the example exhibits the features by marking a "+" or "−" in the appropriate box.

Example

Fifth-grade teacher Amy Peale's students were involved in a study of reptiles. As part of that study the students read *Eyewitness Juniors Amazing Snakes* (Parsons, 1993). After they completed their reading, Amy presented the students with a Semantic Feature Analysis matrix about snakes on the document camera. In the left-hand column, she listed the various types of snakes mentioned in the book, including pythons, cobras, rattlesnakes, milk snakes and vine snakes. Across the top, she listed characteristics of snakes, including "poisonous," "squeezes to kill," "can eat people," and "lays eggs."

Students worked in teams to consider whether each snake listed in the left column possessed the features listed across the top of the page. They checked back in the book to determine the characteristics that each snake possessed. The student discussed their answers while Amy filled in the matrix with pluses and minuses (see below). Following this, she asked students to think about which snakes were most alike and which were most different.

Sample Semantic Feature Analysis Matrix

Type of snake	Poisonous	Squeezes to kill	Can eat people	Lays eggs
python	−	+	+	+
cobra	+	−	−	+
rattlesnake	+	−	−	−
milk snake	−	−	−	+
vine snake	+	−	−	+

References

Anders, P., & Bos, C. (1986). Semantic feature analysis: An interactive strategy for vocabulary development and text comprehension. *Journal of Reading, 20*(7), 610–616.

Parsons, A. (1993). *Eyewitness juniors amazing snakes*. New York: Dorling Kindersley. (I).

Your Turn!

Select a text from the appendix at the end of this book, one of your own choosing, or a newspaper or magazine article mentioning people or concepts that can be compared based on their attributes. Introduce the book. Introduce the Semantic Feature Analysis Matrix on the next page by telling students the names of the concepts to be filled in in the left column and the attributes to be listed across the top. Tell students to think about these concepts and their attributes as they read. When students are finished, they can complete the matrix in pairs.

Semantic Feature Analysis Matrix

Directions: Look at the words in the first column. Then look at the characteristics of each word in the first row. Rate each characteristic with a plus (+) if it is accurate and with a minus (–) if it is not.

Strategy 15

Possible Sentences

GRADE LEVELS: 2–12

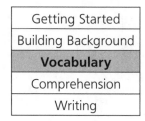

Getting Started
Building Background
Vocabulary
Comprehension
Writing

What Is It?

Possible Sentences (Moore & Moore, 1986) introduces students to new vocabulary words before reading a text at the same time it involves students in predicting text content. Through these experiences, students develop cognitive readiness for reading and heighten their interest in the text to be read.

What Is Its Purpose?

Possible Sentences is a strategy designed to introduce students to unfamiliar vocabulary before they actually read the text. It not only introduces new vocabulary to the students prior to reading, but it helps students activate their prior knowledge about the unfamiliar words by seeing them in context and in relationships to other words in the passage. This strategy is useful for most grade levels and can be used with almost any expository material.

What Do I Do?

1 Select a text appropriate to the level of your students.

2 Identify 7–10 key vocabulary terms from the text. These terms should represent important concepts found in the text. They should include terms that are completely new to the students, as well as those that are familiar.

3 Introduce the terms to the students on the document camera.

4 Ask students to create a sentence that might appear in the text by combining two of the terms into a sentence. Follow this procedure until students have created sentences from all of the words.

5 Ask students to read the selection, keeping in mind the sentences they generated. As they read, they should think about whether the sentences they generated are true based on the text information.

6 After reading, students should evaluate each of the sentences, identifying those that are true or false. They should then change those sentences that are false to conform to the information found in the text.

Example

Fifth-grade teacher Kevin Green's students were involved in a study of space. They were preparing to read a chapter in Sally Ride and Susan Okie's (1995) *To Space & Back*. Prior to having them read, Kevin involved the students in creating Possible Sentences. First, he introduced these words on the document camera: *weightlessness*, *gravity*, *astronaut*, *space sickness*, *orbit*, *shuttle*, *capsule*, and *rocket*. He modeled the procedure first by combining the words *astronaut* and *orbit* into a sentence. The students then created their own sentences. Examples are listed below:

1 The *astronaut* was going to *orbit* the earth.

2 *Space sickness* comes from being confined in the space *capsule*.

3 The space *shuttle* is powered by *rockets*.

4 *Weightlessness* happens because of zero *gravity*.

After reading the passage, the students determined which sentences were actually found in the passage and were accurate based on the information provided. They put check marks next to those sentences that were true. In this instance, they discovered sentence 2 was inaccurate, since space sickness results from weightlessness, not from confinement in the capsule. Students modified this sentence to reflect this fact.

References

Moore, J. W., & Moore, S. A. (1986). Possible sentences. In E. K. Dishner, T. W. Bean, J. E. Readance, & D. W. Moore (Eds.), *Reading in the content areas: Improving classroom instruction* (2nd ed., pp. 196–201). Dubuque, IA: Kendall/Hunt.

Ride, S., & Okie, S. (1995). *To space and back*. New York: Lothrop, Lee & Shepard. (P).

Your Turn!

Try Possible Sentences with a text from the appendix at the end of this book or one of your own choosing. Record key vocabulary terms on the sheet on the next page. Then, form these into sentences. After reading, have students evaluate the accuracy of the sentences and modify those that are incorrect.

Vocabulary Strategies

Possible Sentences

1   **Directions:** Record key terms on these lines:

_____   _____

_____   _____

_____   _____

_____   _____

2   Record possible sentences here. Each sentence must contain two of the words above.

1. _____

2. _____

3. _____

4. _____

5. _____

3   After reading, put a check mark next to the sentences that are true. Change those that are false to make them true.

PART FOUR

Comprehension
Strategies

Three-Minute Pause

GRADE LEVELS: K–12

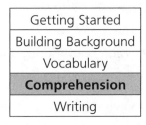

Getting Started
Building Background
Vocabulary
Comprehension
Writing

What Is It?

Because students are inundated with information, there is a good chance that they lack opportunities to reflect upon and process that information. The Three-Minute Pause (Marzano et al., 1992; McTighe & Lyman, 1988) is a strategy that provides students with an opportunity for reflection that can enhance knowledge retention. At strategic points, teachers provide students with the opportunity to pause for 3 minutes, an educational time out. They use this time to reflect on the concepts and ideas that have just been introduced, to make connections to prior knowledge/experience, and/or to seek clarification.

The Three-Minute Pause has many forms; the most popular is "Think–Pair–Share." The idea is to establish a pattern of regular breaks to allow students to process their learning.

What Is Its Purpose?

The purpose of the Three-Minute Pause is to have students negotiate and construct their own meanings about a topic. In order to be critical consumers of information, students must be allowed time to reflect on and verbalize new teachings. The best way for students to learn about a topic is to manipulate it, even if this manipulation occurs inside one's head: Thinking involves the manipulation of ideas, and this strategy provides an excellent opportunity for this to happen.

What Do I Do?

Teachers need to provide students with frequent opportunities to reflect on their learning. Without this reflection time, students may have incomplete knowledge of what is being taught and as such, teachers must often reteach. The Three-Minute Pause is efficient and immediately useful, requiring very little preparation; the teacher just has to deliberately implement it at crucial and relevant points during the text and/or instruction. The steps are as follows:

1 Select and present a text via a read-aloud, document camera, through a Power-Point lecture, and so on.

2 Stop every so often and have the students get into partners or small groups for their Three-Minute Pauses. Use a timer to facilitate this and to also create a sense of urgency and efficiency.

3 First, ask the students to summarize the key points presented thus far. Give them 1 minute to complete this task.

4 Second, ask the students to consider connections to themselves, to other texts, and/or to the world or society at large. Give them 1 minute to complete this task.

5 Third, ask the students to pose questions. Here are some prompts:

- Are there things that are still not clear?
- Are there confusing parts?
- Are you having trouble making connections?
- Can you anticipate where we're headed?
- What do you think are the big ideas?
- Give them 1 minute to complete this task.

6 Present the next segment of information/frontloading and repeat each step. This strategy can be modified in a variety of ways; the most important aspect of the strategy is to have students stop to think about what they are learning. An analogy to consider is the need to "save" when we are working on our computers; our students need a moment to "save" the information you present.

Example

Gene Batchelder is a seventh-grade world history teacher. He taught a unit on Confucianism in which the students had to analyze the influences of Confucianism and changes in Confucian thought during the Sung and Mongol periods.

Gene is very familiar with the Think–Pair–Share strategy (a popular version of the Three-Minute Pause strategy) and used it all the time when he first started teaching. (His credential program and master teacher modeled the strategy constantly; he had never read about it or researched it any further.) However, he found that the longer he taught and the more pressure he felt to address state standards, the less effectively he used this strategy. In order for Think–Pair–Shares to be effective, the teacher must have a specific goal for student learning. Gene had neglected this aspect of the strategy and was having students chitchat in an unfocused, general way about the topic. Although students were given an opportunity to talk and process, they were not fully retaining the information. Because the success of this strategy depends upon explicit instruction, Gene should say, "I would like for you to Think–Pair–Share about how Confucius treated his students."

In his graduate studies, Gene was formally introduced to the Three-Minute Pause in a research article on reading comprehension and realized that he had been using the strategy ineffectively; he preferred the Three-Minute Pause model to Think–Pair–Share because it was more structured. He decided to refocus and reuse the strategy to better instruct his students. He also wanted to be better at talking less so that the students could talk more. A fan of Russell Freedman, he used the informational trade book *Confucius: The Golden Rule* (Freedman, 2002). Using the document camera, Gene presented the text to his students, reading significant excerpts. He would stop and have his students participate in a Three-Minute Pause. During these pauses, he would display his expectations as shown below. He also incorporated sentence starters designed to help those students who had difficulty framing their responses:

Rules for Three-Minute Pauses

First minute: With a partner, think about what you have just learned. Summarize what you have just learned about *Confucius*.

   Prompt: I learned....

Second minute: With a partner, make a connection to yourself, to another text, or to society at large based upon what you have learned.

   Prompt: This reminds me of....

Third minute: Independently, write your question(s) on a piece of paper. You will turn this in at the end of class.

   Prompt: I want to know more about....

Gene modified the Three-Minute Pause; he had the first 2 minutes be an oral discussion with a partner and the last minute was an independent writing activity. He was deliberate in what he wanted his students to do with a partner and what he wanted them to do independently. Gene established this strategy as a routine in his class and his students were able to get a lot of thinking done in 3 minutes.

Gene used a timer and was very consistent about the time. After 3 minutes, he would continue reading the text.

At the end of the class session, Gene would collect the question sheets from each student. He would use that information to evaluate student learning and help him plan for the next class session.

References

Freedman, R. (2002). *Confucius: The golden rule.* New York: Arthur Levine Books. (M).

Marzano, R., Pickering, D., Arredondo, D., Blackburn, G., Brandt, R., & Moffett, C. (1992). *Dimensions of learning teacher's manual.* Alexandria, VA: ASCD.

McTighe, J., & Lyman, F. (1988). Cueing thinking in the classroom: The promise of theory-embedded tools. *Educational Leadership, 45*(7), 18–24.

Your Turn!

Select a text that is pertinent to your topic of study from the appendix at the end of this book, or one of your own choosing. Use the Three-Minute Pause Planning Guide to help you decide where you will pause to check for understanding during the lesson.

Three-Minute Pause Planning Guide

Title of Text _____ Author _____

What key learnings do I want students to get from this text?	1.
	2.
	3.

Three-Minute Pause #1

Where will you pause in the text?

What will students do?

What prompt will you use for this pause?

Three-Minute Pause #2

Where will you pause in the text?

What will students do?

What prompt will you use for this pause?

Three-Minute Pause #3

Where will you pause in the text?

What will students do?

What prompt will you use for this pause?

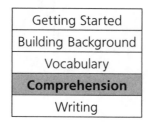

············· **Strategy 17** ·····················

Sticky Notes Bookmark

GRADE LEVELS: K–5

Getting Started
Building Background
Vocabulary
Comprehension
Writing

What Is It?

The Sticky Notes Bookmark strategy (adapted from McLaughlin & Allen, 2002) uses sticky notes for bookmarks and is a way for young students to become active readers instead of passive ones. The strategy focuses young students on making meaning from text by locating four specific things in the text they are reading. Sticky Note Bookmark 1, which is denoted with an exclamation point (!), involves student identification of the most interesting part of the book. Bookmark 2, denoted with a "V," involves student identification of a vocabulary word the class needs to discuss. Bookmark 3, denoted with a question mark (?), involves identification of something the student found confusing. Bookmark 4, denoted with a graphic of a chart, involves identification of an illustration, map, chart, or graph that helped the reader comprehend the text.

What Is Its Purpose?

The purpose of the Sticky Notes Bookmark strategy is to help young readers read with specific goals in mind. By reading to locate specific information, students maintain a clear focus on their reading and identify information that is important to their understanding of the text. This strategy helps students derive understanding from what they read, and moves them beyond simply identifying words to the recognition that they need to construct meaning from what they read.

What Do I Do?

1 Give each student four sticky notes. Explain to students that they will be reading to locate specific information from their text.

2 Demonstrate for students how to label each sticky note. The first bookmark will be labeled with an exclamation point (!) for the most interesting part of the text. The second should be labeled with a "V" for a vocabulary word the class needs to discuss. Bookmark 3 should have a question mark (?) to remind students to identify a confusing part of the text. Bookmark 4 will have a small chart, designed to remind students to look for an illustration, map, chart, or graph that helped them understand the text.

3 Place each labeled Post-it Note on the blackboard. Model for students how to bookmark their texts with sticky notes by reading an informational text and thinking aloud about how you identified and marked with a sticky note an interesting part, a new vocabulary term, a confusing part, and a visual that helped you understand the text.

4 Provide each student with an informational text. Each student can read from the same text or individual students can read from different texts.

5 Involve students in prereading activities related to their texts. These can include KWHL (Strategy 6), Anticipation Guides (Strategy 5), or Table of Contents Prediction (Strategy 8).

6 Have students read independently, bookmarking their texts as they go.

7 After students have finished, have them pair together to share each of their bookmarks.

Example

First-grade teacher Marva Allegro wanted to involve her students in reading more informational texts during independent reading. She had purchased an array of easy-to-read informational texts at appropriate levels for her students including titles from Sundance Publishing and the National Geographic School Publishing.

Marva began her lesson by reviewing with students how to select "just right" informational trade books for independent reading. Once each student had identified a book, she involved them in activating their prior knowledge about the topic of the text by using Table of Contents Predicting (Strategy 8). Through this activity, students gained experience in thinking about the contents of the text they had selected.

Following this activity, Marva distributed four sticky notes to each student. She modeled for students how to code each sticky note bookmark with the codes described earlier. She referred the students to a chart that would remind them what each code meant.

After students had prepared their bookmarks, Marva used the book *An Egg Is Quiet* (Aston, 2006) to model for students how to bookmark their texts with sticky notes. She thought aloud as she read the book to them, noting when she identified parts of the book that addressed each of the sticky notes and modeling how to place the sticky notes on the appropriate places.

After she had finished modeling this process, she gave students the opportunity to look over the books they had selected. She used Table of Contents Prediction (Strategy 8) to involve the students in creating a table of contents for their books and then students worked independently to bookmark the specified sections of the text. After this, students formed teams to share with a partner the places they had bookmarked.

Your Turn!

Select an appropriate text for your students to read from the appendix at the end of this book, or let them select their own text. Use the sample sticky notes on the next page to help students create their own Sticky Note Bookmarks. Model for students how to bookmark text, and then let them perform the task independently.

References

Aston, D. H. (2005) *An egg is quiet.* New York: Chronicle Books. (P).

McLaughlin, M., & Allen, M. B. (2002). *Guided comprehension: A teaching model for grades 3–8.* Newark, DE: International Reading Association.

Sticky Note Bookmarks

!	**v**	
Bookmark 1	Bookmark 2	
Write about an interesting part of book	Write a new vocabulary word	

?		
Bookmark 3	Bookmark 4	
Write about a confusing part of the book	Mark a visual (map, graph, chart, etc.) that helped understanding	

4–3–2–1 Discussion Guide

GRADE LEVELS: 5–12

Getting Started
Building Background
Vocabulary
Comprehension
Writing

What Is It?

The 4–3–2–1 Discussion Guide (adapted from the 3–2–1 Discussion Guide described on Reading Quest (*www.readingquest.org*) serves as a discussion guide for collaborative group work. It requires students to summarize, clarify, and analyze content.

To complete the guide, each group must read a text and then identify and record four new learnings, three comments/opinions, two questions, and one further exploration. New Learnings refer to things that students have learned as a result of reading the text. Comments/Opinions require students to think about how they feel about the new learnings and/or the text; they should consider how the text positions them, which new learning refers to the message of the text, and how they feel about the intended message. The Questions section asks students to state their misunderstanding or need for clarification. Lastly, the section entitled Further Exploration requires students to answer the questions: So what? What does this text mean? How does it relate to society at large?

What Is Its Purpose?

The purpose of the 4–3–2–1 Discussion Guide is to provide students with an opportunity to identify and reflect on key ideas from a text. Students are also asked to use critical literacy to examine the authority of the text by posing questions and comments as well as further explorations.

Through student completion of this activity, the teacher can ascertain where student understandings are incomplete or missing and use their responses to plan instruction and/or discussion topics for the next day. Because the instruction is focused on ideas that students create themselves, the students will be motivated and engaged in the task.

What Do I Do?

This strategy is best used for collaborative groups of four to six members. The teacher may want to model this strategy first by performing a think-aloud for the entire class. You might want to read a short passage and demonstrate your responses for the 4–3–2–1 Discussion Guide. You may also want to provide sentence frames or prompts depending on the class level. The following chart provides some guiding questions and prompts:

Guiding Questions and Prompts	
4 **New** **Learnings**	What did you learn from the text? What new facts did you learn? What are some things that you didn't know about prior to reading this text? What did you find interesting? *Sample prompts:* I learned _____. It was interesting how _____.
3 **Comments/** **Opinions**	What did you think about _____? What did you think about the author's message? How did you feel when _____? What would you change? Did you agree or disagree with something mentioned in the text? Did something surprise you? What textual connections can you make? *Sample prompts:* I think _____. I felt _____. I was surprised when _____. This reminded me of _____.
2 **Questions**	What do you want to know more about? What did you find confusing? *Sample prompts:* Why did _____? What is _____?
1 **Further** **Exploration**	Is there anything that needs to be clarified or studied more? What other topics did this text make you think about? What's the next step? What does this text mean in the larger context? *Sample prompts:* I want to learn more about _____. The author's next step should be _____.

The following steps can guide the use of this strategy:

1 Select a text that addresses the topic of study. Have all students read the text prior to meeting in their groups. This can be assigned for homework or read in class.

2 Assign groups and roles, especially a recorder to write down the group's responses. Other possible roles include a facilitator to ask the questions and guide the discussion, a timekeeper to manage the time, and a reporter to share out loud to the group.

3 Have the recorder write down the topic and title of the text.

4 Have students talk in their groups to complete the 4–3–2–1 Chart. Optional: Have the reporter share with the whole class.

5 Collect the templates and use the information to guide future instruction.

Note that the template provided is merely a suggestion. This strategy can be adapted in many different ways depending upon what you're teaching. For example, if you are studying the transition from communism to democracy, you might have students write down four new vocabulary words they learned, three differences between communism and democracy, two similarities, and one question they still may have.

Example

Mr. Buddy Gray teaches 10th-grade English. His students just finished reading John Steinbeck's (1939) *The Grapes of Wrath*. Based on their responses in class discussions, he learned that his students did not know very much about the Dust Bowl. So, he wanted to contextualize Steinbeck's book by having the students read some expository text about the subject. He felt that they needed to understand the historical context of the novel in order to fully comprehend it. So, for homework, he had them read Jerry Stanley's (1993) *Children of the Dust Bowl: The True Story of the School at Weedpatch Camp*.

Mr. Gray distributed the 4–3–2–1 Discussion Guide and had the students work in small groups to complete the guide. Then, as a whole class, he led them in creating a text-to-text connection by having them complete a Venn Diagram (Strategy 25), comparing and contrasting Steinbeck's and Stanley's depictions of the Dust Bowl in the two texts.

In reading the students' responses, Mr. Gray discovered that they were making personal connections between past (Dust Bowl, Great Depression, migration) and current events (economic downturn, border issues). For example, several groups recorded in the Comments/Opinions section how much the Great Depression reminded them of today's recession because "people were losing their homes and jobs." Other students wrote about migration and immigration; they recorded responses such as "The Okies moving out West for a better life reminded me of my family immigrating to America. Both groups had to deal with hardships and prejudices." Students were clearly connecting their current lived experiences to the texts. As a result, Mr. Gray modified his lesson for that week to include discussions about these topics in addition to an explicit lesson comparing and contrasting past and present national policies on the economy and immigration. He wanted to use what the students were already interested in and to expand their knowledge.

References

Reading Quest: Making sense of social studies. Retrieved from *www.readingquest.org.*
Stanley, J. (1993). *Children of the dust bowl: The true story of the school at Weedpatch Camp.* New York: Crown Books for Young Readers. (M).
Steinbeck, J. (1939). *The grapes of wrath.* New York: Penguin Classics. (YA).

Your Turn!

Select a text pertinent to your topic of study from the appendix at the end of this book, or one of your own choosing. Using the document camera, model via a think-aloud with the whole class each of the four steps of the 4–3–2–1 Discussion Guide. Then, choose another text on the same topic and have students work in small groups to complete the guide.

4-3-2-1 Discussion Guide

Directions: Complete the form below.

Topic:
Text:

4 New Learnings	1. 2. 3. 4.
3 Comments/ Opinions	1. 2. 3.
2 Questions	1. 2.
1 Further Exploration	1.

Four-Box Comment Card

GRADE LEVELS: 3–12

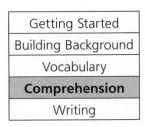

| Getting Started |
| Building Background |
| Vocabulary |
| **Comprehension** |
| Writing |

What Is It?

The Four-Box Comment Card (adapted from Vacca & Vacca, 2008) is a template for guiding small-group discussions of informational texts. The teacher provides four thinking prompts, one for each square. Each prompt requires students to think about the text in a slightly different way; for example, the prompts that appear in each of the boxes might include one comment, one surprise, one question, or one observation. This is the most popular format for this strategy and it is shown in the example described below.

Small groups convene to discuss a particular text, using this template as a guide. In their small groups, they will have the opportunity to practice consensus-building skills in addition to other important discussion skills, such as turn taking, respect-fully disagreeing, and so on. A recorder writes down the group's responses and the reporter shares the responses with the whole class. Instead of small groups, this template can also be used to solicit individual responses; in this way, this strategy can also be used as an assessment.

Furthermore, this strategy is easily adaptable to most grade and ability levels and all content areas. For example, for secondary students, we suggest employing prompts that address critical literacy. Essential questions like the following can help teachers:

1 Who constructs the texts whose representations are dominant in a particular culture at a particular time?

2 How do readers become complicit with the persuasive ideologies of texts?

3 Whose interests are served by such representations and readings?

4 How can readers reconstruct inequitable texts and readings? (Morgan, 1997)

One of the samples at the end of this section shows how we adapted these questions for the Four-Box Comment Card strategy. Also, the chart below clarifies these prompts in more detail:

Prompt	Explanation
1. Who constructs the texts whose representations are dominant in a particular culture at a particular time?	Have the students consider the author's perspective, the author's position, and the author's message. Does the author present a dominant viewpoint that is accepted by the mainstream? If so, why? Also, the students can consider funding sources, research institutions, etc. *Suggested prompt:* Who is the author? How does his or her point of view show in the text?
2. How do readers become complicit with the persuasive ideologies of texts?	Have students consider their positions, or rather, opinions in regard to the text's message(s). Have them think about how the author is persuading them. What rhetorical or literary devices are being used? How is the author attempting to appeal to the readers? *Suggested prompt:* What are the messages the author wants you to accept? Do you agree or disagree with the author?
3. Whose interests are served by such representations and readings?	Have students consider the targeted audiences. Who is the author trying to persuade and why? And, who is the author writing on behalf of? Who is benefiting? *Suggested prompt:* Whose interests are served by this text? Who benefits? How?
4. How can readers reconstruct inequitable texts and readings?	Have students reconsider whether or not they agree with the message and how they would change the meaning or desired outcomes of this text to fit their own system of beliefs. What would they delete? What new information would they add? How would they make the text more balanced? This part addresses personal agency and social action. *Suggested prompt:* How would you change the desired outcome or meaning of this text?

For teachers new to implementing critical literacy, we suggest applying these prompts to an advertisement and then moving on to informational texts. This particular Four-Box Comment Card will require a whole-class discussion with teacher scaffolding in order maximize effectiveness.

We would like to direct the reader to the samples provided at the end of this section; we have provided more examples of prompts to suit a variety of levels and purposes.

What Is Its Purpose?

In addition to guiding small-group discussions, the purpose of the Four-Box Comment Card is to encourage students to assume a position about a text, aligning with the tenets of critical literacy. Critical literacy encourages readers and consumers to not passively accept the status quo, but to examine the underlying dynamics at play and to assume one of three stances toward the text:

1 The dominant stance in which one accepts the message.

2 The negotiated stance in which one disputes a particular claim but accepts the overall message.

3 The oppositional stance in which one rejects the message (Apple, 1992).

Through the Four-Box Comment Card, students are introduced to multiple perspectives and are encouraged to not passively rely on authoritative interpretations. Most importantly, students are asked to think critically and to express their opinions.

What Do I Do?

This is an easy strategy to implement, requiring very little preparation but when used correctly, yielding great results. Students learn how to critically think about a text and are exposed to multiple perspectives about the same text.

1 Select an informational text that is slightly controversial and/or has potential for dissenting viewpoints. For example, a text about tree frogs would not be effective; however, a text about the effects of deforestation on the habitats of tree frogs would be.

2 Select which prompts you would like to use. Consider the levels of your students, the amount of prior knowledge they have, and the text you are using. Some of the samples provided in this section can be employed for any and all texts; some, like the critical literacy prompts, require particular texts. We suggest completing the Four-Box Comment Card yourself before disseminating to your students.

3 Assign the reading prior to implementing this activity. (Having students read the text for homework works well.)

4 Organize students into groups of four to six members. Have them select a reporter and a recorder. (You could also have them select other roles: timekeeper, facilitator, and so on.)

5 Have the reporter fold a piece of paper vertically and then horizontally to create four boxes.

6 Display your chosen prompts via overhead, chart paper, document camera, and so on. Have the reporter write the prompts in each box.

7 Give each group 10–15 minutes to discuss the prompts. (You might want to establish norms for the discussion prior to this.)

8 Have each group come to a consensus about each prompt. Then, have the reporter record the groups' position.

9 Have the reporter share with the groups. (If a document camera is available, you can have the reporter project the Four-Box Comment Card so that everyone can follow along.)

10 Optional: You could record the responses on a master template and compile the results to create a class opinion. Again, this would be a further extension of negotiating opinions and arriving at a consensus.

Example

Eleventh-grade American history teacher Felix Fortmann complains of having too many texts that need to be read in a short amount of time. He acknowledges that he does not have enough time in the school year to review all the texts, which are mainly expository, that he requires his students to read. As a result, he uses the Four-Box Comment Card as a means of providing his students with an opportunity to deconstruct the text in a short time period.

During a unit on World War II that focused on Executive Order 9066, which required an Internet search of Japanese Americans, he had his students read Ellen Levine's (1995) *A Fence Away from Freedom*, which consists of oral histories of Japanese American interns combined with Levine's commentaries and historical analyses. Felix wanted the students to more fully understand the personal experiences of Japanese Americans during the war in order to build personal connections. The essential question for the unit was How does war affect people? Prior to this reading assignment, Felix reviewed primary source documents such as Executive Order 9066 and Roosevelt's "Day of Infamy" speech in response to the attack on Pearl Harbor that marked the official entrance of the United States into World War II. He assigned the Levine book for homework.

When the students came into class the next day, Felix knew that he only had about 20 minutes to devote to this text. The Four-Box Comment Card strategy provided a creative way of allowing the students to have critical discussions where their voices are heard and at the same time, maximizing the use of precious class time.

Felix counted off his students and placed them into five groups. He had index cards with roles labeled on them. The students chose a card and were assigned to one of the following roles:

1 The recorder, who would be responsible for writing the group's answers to the prompts.

2 The reporter, who would be responsible for sharing the group's thoughts with the larger group.

3 The timekeeper, who would be responsible for managing time.

4 The facilitator, who would be responsible for asking the prompts.

5 The fact checker, who would be responsible for referring to the text to find or confirm details.

6 The mediator, who would be responsible for making sure group members are respectful.

Then, Felix placed a blank copy of the Four-Box Comment Card on the document camera and had the recorder write down the prompts (see sample for his prompts and for student responses). He set a timer for 10 minutes and walked around as groups were instructed to discuss their prompts and to come to a consensus for each prompt, which the recorder was to write down and the reporter was to share with the whole class. Felix monitored and interjected as needed. A sample of one group's Four-Box Comment Card is provided below:

Sample Four-Box Comment Card

One comment:	One surprise:
• All these stories are so sad! They clearly show how racist Americans were even before Pearl Harbor, which was just an excuse.	• Many Japanese Americans remained loyal to the United States, even volunteering for the all-Nisei 442nd Regimental Combat Team. (We wouldn't do that if we were forced to live in concentration camps for no reason.) Why weren't they angry and resentful?

One question:	One observation:
• Why didn't Americans protest this? • We want to know more about the Japanese Peruvians who were brought to the U.S. camps.	• The U.S. government forced more than 110,000 Japanese Americans from their homes along the West Coast and made them live in "relocation camps," which are like the Nazi concentration camps. These camps were poorly constructed.

After 8 minutes, Felix called on the timekeepers to move their groups along. After 10 minutes, he gave each group's reporter 2 minutes to present to the entire group, projecting their Four-Box Comment Card on the document camera. (The timekeeper is responsible for signaling to the reporter when his or her 2 minutes are up.)

After all the groups shared, Felix gave each student another opportunity to voice his or her opinion via a 5-minute quickwrite. His prompts were (1) What is your opinion of Levine's book? and (2) How did the group discussions influence your opinion? Felix collected the quickwrites and the templates and used them as a way to assess student understanding of the material.

References

Apple, M. W. (1992). The text and cultural politics. *Educational Researcher, 21*(7), 4–11, 19.

Levine, E. (1995). *A fence away from freedom*. New York: Putnam Juvenile. (M).

Morgan, W. (1997). *Critical literacy in the classroom: The art of the possible*. New York: Routledge.

Vacca, R. T., & Vacca, J. L. (2007). *Content area reading: Literacy and learning across the curriculum* (9th ed.). Boston: Allyn & Bacon.

Your Turn!

Select an informational trade book on the particular topic of study from the appendix at the end of this book, or one of your own choosing. Make sure you use a text and topic that has the potential for a good discussion. Choose a Four-Box Comment Card from the samples provided on the next page or create your own. Consider the level of your students and their prior knowledge in designing the four prompts.

Possible Templates for Four-Box Comment Cards

Directions: Complete the cards below.

One comment:	One surprise:
	I like …
One question:	**One observation:**
	I wonder …

One comment:	One surprise:
	I did not like …
One question:	**One observation:**
	I would change …

1. Who is the author? How does his or her point of view show in the text?	2. What are the messages the author wants you to accept? Do you agree or disagree with the author?
	I agree with:
3. Whose interests are served by this text? Who benefits? How?	**4. How would you change the desired outcome or meaning of this text?**
	I disagree with:

1.	2.
	I agree with reservations:
3.	**4.**
	I need more information: OR I would like to further explore:

Discussion Web

GRADE LEVELS: 3–12

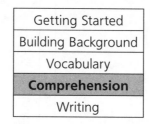

| Getting Started |
| Building Background |
| Vocabulary |
| **Comprehension** |
| Writing |

What Is It?

Discussion Webs (Alvermann, 1991) are graphic aids that help students think critically about what they have read. This organizer presents students with a central question to consider, along with spaces where readers can fill in supporting evidence in the "Yes" column, indicating agreement with the key question, or in the "No" column, indicating disagreement with the key question.

What Is Its Purpose?

Discussion Webs encourage students to consider different points of view about an issue, helping them to reflect on the fact that there are multiple ways to view a particular idea. This ability to take multiple perspectives in relation to an idea is an important aspect of critical literacy. The Discussion Web forces students to not only support their own opinion about an issue, but also provide support for the opposing point of view. In this way, the Discussion Web helps to keep discussions focused and ensures that students support their viewpoints with relevant information.

What Do I Do?

The steps in using Discussion Webs are as follows:

1 Engage students in prereading activities related to an informational text.

2 After students have read, introduce the central question, writing it on the Discussion Web. Explain the format of the web, which includes two columns, one on the right side of the question and one on the left. The left-hand column is the "Yes" column; this is where students record their reasons for disagreeing with the central question. The right-hand column is the "No" column. This is where students record their reasons for agreeing with the central question.

3 Put students in pairs to review the text, using sticky notes to identify three reasons they agree with the central question and three reasons they disagree.

4 Ask students to record these reasons in each of the two support columns on the web.

5 Ask students to combine partners to create groups of four. Each of the four students should present at least one reason in support of the question and one in opposition to the question to the rest of the group. This ensures that each student participates. The group of four compares their Discussion Webs and reaches a group conclusion. Dissenters may develop a minority report.

6 Each group presents its single best conclusion to the class and any dissenting opinions. Finally, the teacher opens up the discussion to the entire class.

Example

Middle school English teacher Alvin Sang was interested in helping his students develop critical literacy skills by engaging them in reflecting on their use of online literacy both in and out of class. He then introduced the students to an article from *The New York Times* online entitled "Literacy Debate: Online RU Really Reading" (*www.nytimes.com/2008/07/27/books/27reading.html*). This persuasive essay examines the nature of online reading and raises a number of interesting questions about whether or not online reading is equivalent to more traditional forms of reading and contributes to the development of reading abilities. Prior to reading, Alvin involved students in a brief discussion of the ways in which they use reading as they engage with electronic texts. He explained that the article explores both sides of the debate around the question of whether or not online reading is as valuable as other forms of reading. Alvin then filled in the center of the Discussion Web with the question "Does online reading contribute to the development of reading skills students need for success in the 21st century?" He asked students to think about this question as they read the article.

Alvin introduced the Discussion Web strategy on an overhead, showing students how the web organizer asks them to consider a central question and list reasons for responding affirmatively to the question and reasons for responding negatively. He explained that they should be able to identify and record at least three reasons for answering "yes" to the central question and three reasons for answering "no." In other words, they were supposed to consider both sides of the issue. He instructed students to use sticky notes to write down examples for and against the central question within the article.

After reading the article, Alvin had students complete their webs in teams. A sample completed organizer is found below. After this, each group reported to the larger group on the reasons they listed on both sides of the web. A lively discussion ensued, with students arguing for their positions. Finally, students reached a consensus about their thoughts on online reading.

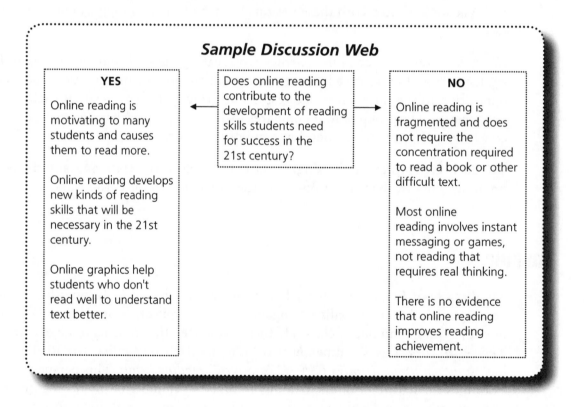

Sample Discussion Web

YES

Online reading is motivating to many students and causes them to read more.

Online reading develops new kinds of reading skills that will be necessary in the 21st century.

Online graphics help students who don't read well to understand text better.

Does online reading contribute to the development of reading skills students need for success in the 21st century?

NO

Online reading is fragmented and does not require the concentration required to read a book or other difficult text.

Most online reading involves instant messaging or games, not reading that requires real thinking.

There is no evidence that online reading improves reading achievement.

References

Alvermann, D. (1991). The discussion web: A graphic aid to learning across the curriculum. *The Reading Teacher, 45,* 92–99.

Rich, M. (2008, July 27). Literacy debate: Online RU really reading. *New York Times.* Retrieved from *www.nytimes.com/2008/07/27/books/27reading.html.*

Your Turn!

Select a book or text that addresses a controversial topic or issue that students may have strong opinions about. Select a text from the appendix at the end of this book, or one of your own choosing. Using the Discussion Web on the next page, introduce the and explain the question you want students to think about as they read. Write this question in the center box. Then let them form groups to discuss and record their opinions about the two sides of the question or issue. Have them record at least three reasons for their opinions on the two sides of the web. Then discuss their responses as a group.

Discussion Web about _____

Directions: Complete the organizer below.

YES		NO
	→ ←	

Data Chart

GRADE LEVELS: K–12

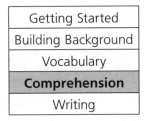

| Getting Started |
| Building Background |
| Vocabulary |
| **Comprehension** |
| Writing |

What Is It?

A Data Chart can help students organize information about a given subject. It allows them to organize content-related information from informational trade books, magazines, or newspapers. Data Charts provide an easy-to-read overview of complex data from multiple sources. That makes it possible for students to access information at a glance.

What Is Its Purpose?

The purpose of a Data Chart is to help students see data from multiple sources and compare and contrast that data. Completion of a Data Chart requires that students first categorize information and then compare and contrast information. In this way, they can form conclusions based on the data displayed on the visual organizer.

What Do I Do?

1 Select an appropriate book, magazine, or newspaper on a topic of interest to your students.

2 Determine the characteristics of the topic that you want students to focus on.

3 Create a Data Chart (see example below). List the topic characteristics across the top of each column of the chart.

4 List the examples of the topic in the rows on the left side of the chart.

5 Help students locate the information and then complete the chart with words or pictures.

Example

Sixth-grade teacher Cheryl Shanahan involved her students in the study of explorers. They enjoyed reading *The Picture History of Great Explorers* (Clements, 2009), an entertaining book that provides information in an engaging format about a variety of explorers. After students completed the book, Cheryl created a Data Chart on large chart paper to help students retrieve and reflect upon information about the various explorers and their discoveries. She listed the following aspects of the discoveries across the top of the grid: "Name," "Method of exploration," "Nationality," "Discovery," and "When?" She then listed the names of the following explorers down the left side of the chart: Leif Eriksson, Christopher Columbus, Ferdinand Magellan, and James Cook (see example below). Students then worked in teams to complete the cells of the chart, looking back in the book to confirm their answers. Following this, Cheryl recorded their answers on the larger chart in the front of the room. She then asked students to identify similarities and differences about the explorers, as well as conclusions they might draw about their discoveries.

Sample Data Chart for Explorers

Name	Method of exploration	Nationality	Discovery	When?
Leif Eriksson	Ship	Greenlander	Vinland (Newfoundland)	1001
Christopher Columbus	Ship	Spanish	San Salvador	1492
Ferdinand Magellan	Ship	Portuguese	Pacific Ocean	1549
James Cook	Ship	British	Australia, New Zealand	1768

References

Clements, G. (2009). *The picture history of great explorers*. New York: Frances Lincoln. (I).

Your Turn!

Select a text from the appendix at the back of this book, or one of your own choosing. List characteristics of the topic across the top of the chart and examples of the topic down the left side of the chart. For example, if students are comparing types of whales, list the characteristics of whales across the top of the chart and the types of whales down the left side of the chart. Then ask students to fill in the chart, using words or pictures.

Comprehension Strategies

Data Chart for _____

Directions: Complete the chart below.

Study Guide

GRADE LEVELS: 3–12

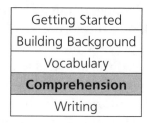

| Getting Started |
| Building Background |
| Vocabulary |
| **Comprehension** |
| Writing |

What Is It?

A Study Guide (Herber, 1978; Vacca & Vacca, 2008) provides a way for teachers to guide students through content-related text. It helps students to distinguish important information from unimportant information and to focus on content the teacher considers critical. It allows the teacher to pose questions and provide students with guidance during a reading task.

What Is Its Purpose?

The purpose of a Study Guide is for the teacher to support student learning by providing questions for students to answer that guide them through the text. The questions provided help students identify important information that is crucial to their overall understanding of the content.

What Do I Do?

1 Select a piece of content-related text.

2 Identify the information in the text that you consider to be most crucial to student understanding.

3 Develop a series of questions designed to guide students through the text. Indicate the page numbers on which the answers to the questions can be located.

4 Ask students to complete the Study Guide as they read the assigned text.

5 Discuss the students' answers to the questions on the guide after they have completed it.

Example

High school science teacher Tim Goodspan's students were studying reptiles. During this time, an interesting article entitled "Beware: Don't Tread on 'Em: Spring Brings Serpents out of Hibernation" appeared in *The San Diego Union Tribune* about the dangers posed by rattlesnakes in the spring.

Tim helped the students preview the article, showing them the headings and the large graphic that accompanied the article. He first introduced the text, asking students to reflect on the meaning of the title "Beware: Don't Tread on 'Em." To guide his students' reading of this informative article, he presented them with a Study Guide designed to focus their learning as they made their way through the text. Tim then distributed the Study Guide, asking students to complete it as they read the article (see sample below). The students completed the guide as they read, and after they finished their reading they formed pairs. Each pair of students compared their answers, checking for accuracy. Students later used the Study Guides again as they prepared for the chapter test.

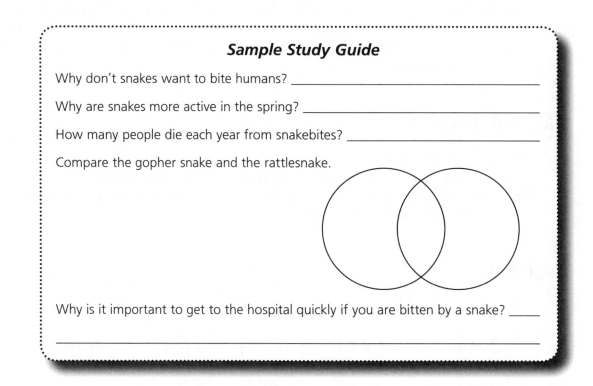

Sample Study Guide

Why don't snakes want to bite humans? _____

Why are snakes more active in the spring? _____

How many people die each year from snakebites? _____

Compare the gopher snake and the rattlesnake.

Why is it important to get to the hospital quickly if you are bitten by a snake? _____

_____

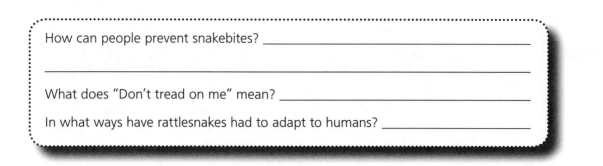

How can people prevent snakebites? _____

_____

What does "Don't tread on me" mean? _____

In what ways have rattlesnakes had to adapt to humans? _____

References

Herber, H. (1978). *Teaching reading in the content areas.* Englewood Cliffs, NJ: Prentice-Hall.

Stetz, M. (2002, April 22). Beware: Don't tread on 'em. *San Diego Union Tribune.* Retrieved from *www.pqasb.pqarchiver.com/sandiego-sub/access/115647024.html?FMT=FT&.*

Vacca, R., & Vacca, J. (2007). *Content area reading* (9th ed.). Boston: Allyn & Bacon.

Your Turn!

Involve your students in reading an appropriate informational text. Select a text from the appendix at the end of this book, or one of your own choosing. For middle school and high school students, you may wish to use the copy of the newspaper article entitled "Beware: Don't Tread on 'Em" that can be found on the Internet. You can fill in the Study Guide template with the questions suggested above, or you may wish to create your own questions.

Study Guide for _____

_____

Directions: Use the pages indicated to locate the answers to the questions listed below.

p. _____ **1.** _____

p. _____ **2.** _____

p. _____ **3.** _____

p. _____ **4.** _____

p. _____ **5.** _____

p. _____ **6.** _____

p. _____ **7.** _____

Semantic Map

GRADE LEVELS: K–12

Getting Started
Building Background
Vocabulary
Comprehension
Writing

What Is It?

The five most common expository text patterns include description, sequence, comparison–contrast, cause–effect, and problem–solution. Just as fictional stories follow a pattern that includes characters, setting, and plot, expository texts typically follow one of these five patterns. All of these patterns may appear on a single page of text.

The next five strategies, which include Semantic Maps, Series of Events Chart (Strategy 24), Venn Diagrams (Strategy 25), Cause–Effect Maps (Strategy 25), and Problem–Solution Outlines (Strategy 27), are all ways to help students recognize and comprehend these five patterns.

A Semantic Map (Heimlich & Pittelman, 1986) is a visual organizer that can help students organize information from an expository passage that is written in a descriptive mode. This text type usually describes a person, place, thing, or object. There are no specific signal words associated with this text structure.

Semantic Maps help students visualize relationships between concepts. These concepts typically include the *class* the key word falls into, the *properties* of that class, and *examples* of those properties. In the example below, the word *bats* would fall into the class of mammal, the properties of bats would include what they look like (appearance), where they live (habitat), and what they eat (diet). The words listed under each property represent examples. In addition, Semantic Maps can be

◆ 113 ◆

used before and/or after reading as a way to familiarize students with important vocabulary and concepts found in a particular text.

What Is Its Purpose?

The purpose of a Semantic Map is to help students organize descriptive information. Semantic Maps are easy to construct and provide a way for students to cluster words in ways that mimic the way information is arranged in the memory. The maps provide a visual representation of the way in which the author chose to organize the text. Through this experience, students become familiar with the concepts found in the text, but more importantly they increase their understanding of description as a pattern of organization for expository text.

What Do I Do?

1 To create a Semantic Map before students read, the teacher first selects a text with a clear organization, preferably in a descriptive pattern. Then the teacher presents the concept to be studied and writes that term in the "bubble" in the center of the web.

2 Ask students to brainstorm words related to that term.

3 Students might then categorize these terms, and indicate these categories or properties of the concept in the square boxes on the map. For younger students or struggling readers, the teacher can provide the categories for the students. The teacher might choose to use the headings found in the book as the categories.

4 After completing their reading, students add additional examples of each property to the Semantic Map. They may just add facts to the existing properties, or they may add new properties to the map. Many teachers like to record this newly acquired information on the map using a different colored pen or marker. In this way, students can compare what they knew before they read with what they added after reading.

Example

The example below illustrates a semantic map that a third-grade class developed after reading *Zipping, Zapping, Zooming Bats* (Earle, 2009). Their teacher Dan O'Brien wanted the students to begin to understand the expository structure of description. Prior to their reading, Dan presented them with a Semantic Map that displayed the name of the book, *Bats*, in the central circle. He provided the headings found in the book. Before reading, the students listed what they already know about each of the categories. These are shown below in the example. They were then asked to read for the purpose of locating descriptive details related to each of these categories. After reading, the students worked in teams to fill in additional details related to each category. An important skill, not to be overlooked, is teaching students how to refer back to the text to find and/or confirm answers. In order to complete a Semantic Map, students will need to refer back to the text frequently. Their responses are in **bold** print in the sample below.

This activity could also serve as a springboard for writing. Using this Semantic Map, students can write their own expository texts: specifically, informative or descriptive paragraphs.

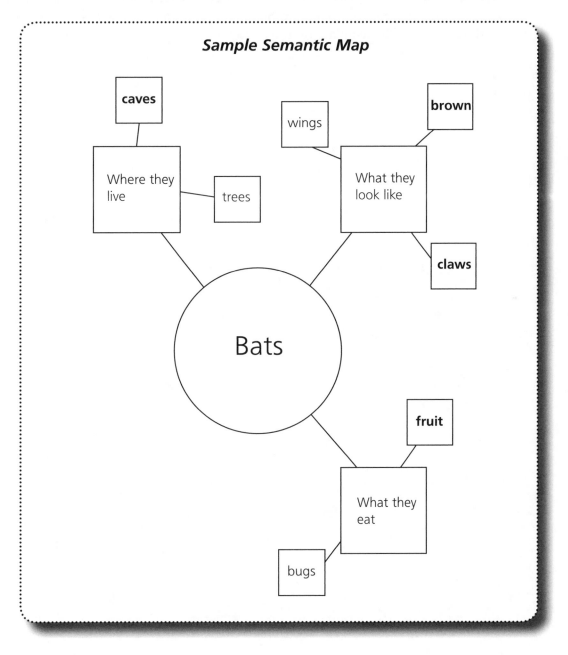

Sample Semantic Map

References

Earle, A. (2009). *Zipping, zapping, zooming bats*. New York: Collins. (P).

Heimlich, S. D., & Pittelman, J. D. (1986). *Semantic mapping: Classroom applications*. Newark, DE: International Reading Association.

Your Turn!

Choose a text from the appendix at the end of this book that uses a descriptive structure, or select a section from a trade book or textbook that uses this pattern. Involve your students in creating a Semantic Map that represents the organization of the text using the template on the next page.

Comprehension Strategies

Semantic Map

Directions: Complete the Semantic Map below.

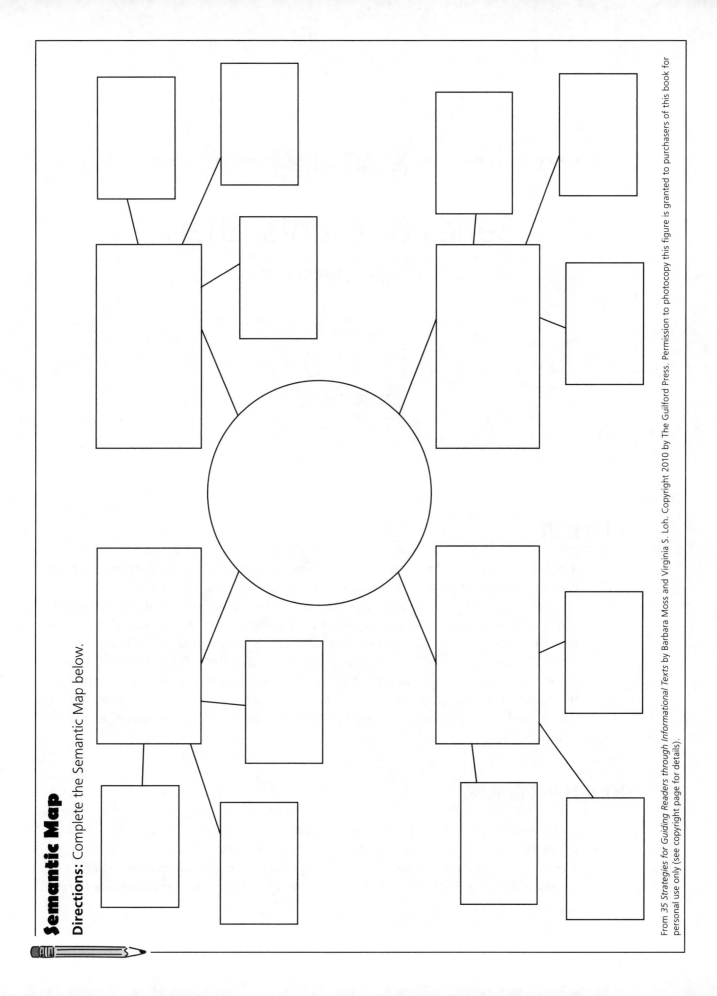

Series of Events Chart

GRADE LEVELS: K–12

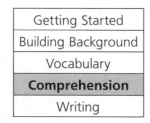

Getting Started
Building Background
Vocabulary
Comprehension
Writing

What Is It?

The Series of Events Chart is a visual organizer designed to help students understand the expository text pattern of sequencing. Sequencing is one of the most common of all expository text patterns and one of the easiest to teach. Authors often use sequential order to organize facts, events, or concepts. The sequence pattern is also used to provide directions for making or doing something. Signal words like *first, second, third, then, next, last, before, after,* and *finally* indicate the order of events. It is easy for students to grasp this pattern because they are familiar with this structure as it appears in narrative. Following a text's sequence is necessary to understanding simple trade books as well as more sophisticated texts such as newspaper or magazine articles.

What Is Its Purpose?

The Series of Events Chart helps students reflect on a sequence of events, steps in a process, and so on by recording these events in order on a graphic organizer. Like a timeline, a Series of Events Chart helps students focus on chronological order, a commonly found pattern in expository text. The ability to comprehend different text structures such as comparison–contrast is an important aspect of critical literacy. Those students who can identify text structures are more able to comprehend texts than those who cannot.

What Do I Do?

1 Select a text that reflects a sequential organizational pattern.

2 Discuss the idea of sequence, explaining that we use sequences in everyday life. For example, when we get up in the morning we follow a particular sequence as we get ready to face the day.

3 Present students with the Series of Events Chart.

4 Ask students to read carefully to note the sequence of events in the text. Have them note signal words like *first, second, third,* and so on.

5 After they have read, ask students to work in teams to complete the Series of Events Chart.

Example

Seventh-grade science teacher Elaine Carter's students were studying mitosis. Using a section of the textbook that outlined this process, she created a lesson plan designed to make students aware of the sequence of events that occurs during mitosis. She began the lesson by asking students to consider how cell division might occur. She recorded their responses on the board. On the overhead Elaine then showed students an example of a sequentially organized paragraph using signal words like *first, second, then, after,* and so on. She encouraged students to look for these signal words to guide them through the passage in the textbook detailing the stages in the process of mitosis. At this point she distributed copies of a Series of Events Chart. Students read the passage silently and recorded key events in order on the chart (see below). Following completion of the series of events, they then formed teams to compare answers. Each team shared their answers with the entire group. Finally, students wrote about the questions they still had about the process in their learning logs.

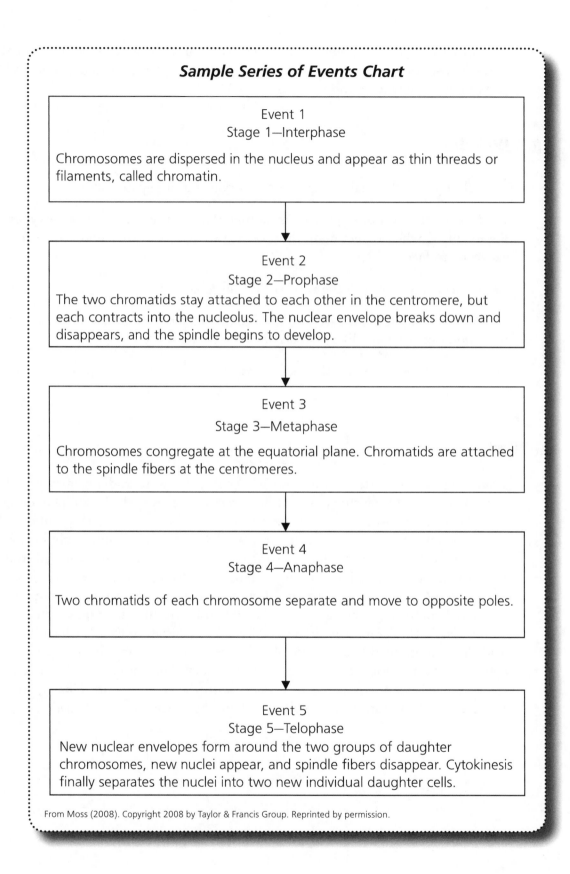

Sample Series of Events Chart

Event 1
Stage 1—Interphase

Chromosomes are dispersed in the nucleus and appear as thin threads or filaments, called chromatin.

Event 2
Stage 2—Prophase
The two chromatids stay attached to each other in the centromere, but each contracts into the nucleolus. The nuclear envelope breaks down and disappears, and the spindle begins to develop.

Event 3
Stage 3—Metaphase

Chromosomes congregate at the equatorial plane. Chromatids are attached to the spindle fibers at the centromeres.

Event 4
Stage 4—Anaphase

Two chromatids of each chromosome separate and move to opposite poles.

Event 5
Stage 5—Telophase
New nuclear envelopes form around the two groups of daughter chromosomes, new nuclei appear, and spindle fibers disappear. Cytokinesis finally separates the nuclei into two new individual daughter cells.

From Moss (2008). Copyright 2008 by Taylor & Francis Group. Reprinted by permission.

References

Moss, B. (2008). Facts that matter: Teaching students to read informational text. In D. Lapp, J. Flood, & N. Farnan (Eds.), *Content area reading and learning: Instructional strategies* (pp. 209–236). New York: Erlbaum.

Your Turn!

Identify a section from a textbook, a trade book, or a newspaper article that is clearly organized in a sequential pattern. Select a text from the appendix at the end of the book, or one of your own choosing. Introduce the Series of Events Chart and associated signal words to your students. Direct them to read to note the order of events in the text. Then let them work in pairs to complete the chart.

Series of Events Chart

Directions: List each of the events in one of the boxes provided. Be sure that you put them in the correct order.

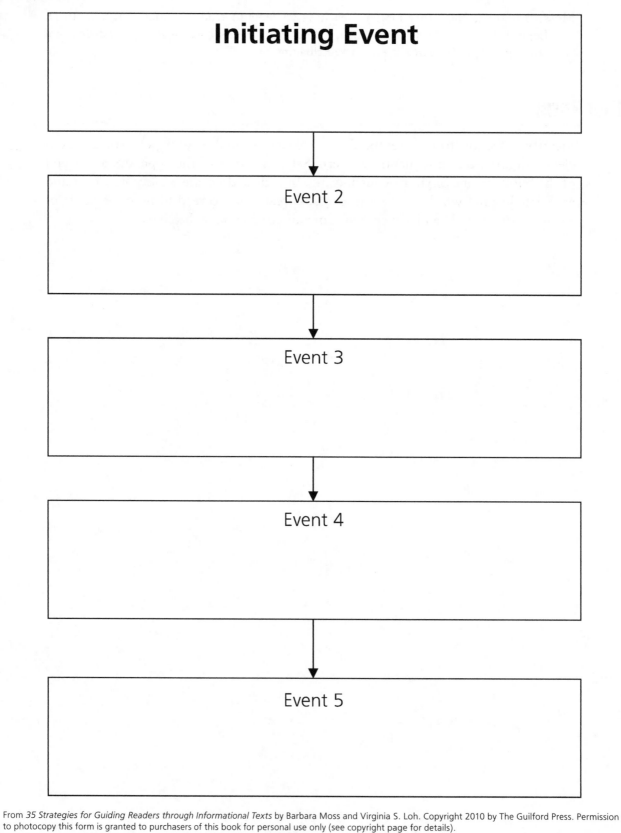

Initiating Event

Event 2

Event 3

Event 4

Event 5

Venn Diagram

GRADE LEVELS: K–12

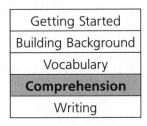

| Getting Started |
| Building Background |
| Vocabulary |
| **Comprehension** |
| Writing |

What Is It?

A Venn Diagram is a visual organizer designed to demonstrate the organizational pattern of comparison and contrast. This pattern is often found in informational texts. Signal words like *alike, different from,* and *on the other hand* are often used to alert readers to this text type. A Venn Diagram is a visual often used in the study of mathematics. It is comprised of two overlapping circles. It illustrates similarities and differences between concepts, ideas, events, or people. Differences are listed on each of the circles; similarities are indicated on the overlapping area of the two circles. In this way, it helps students develop understanding of comparison and contrast text structures.

What Is Its Purpose?

The purpose of the Venn Diagram is to focus student thinking on the comparison and contrast of ideas as a text structure. It provides a visual representation of information provided in a text that employs the pattern of comparison–contrast.

What Do I Do?

1 Locate a text that requires students to compare and/or contrast two things.

2 Introduce a copy of the Venn Diagram on the overhead or document camera. Introduce the concepts of comparison–contrast to the students by comparing objects from everyday life (e.g., day and night, summer and winter).

3 Locate a text that uses the comparison–contrast pattern. Identify ideas, concepts, or people that are compared in the text. Point out to students the use of signal words such as *alike*, *similar to*, and *different from*.

4 Explain to students that they need to think about the similarities and differences between these two important ideas, concepts, or people.

5 Have students read the text. Then distribute copies of the Venn Diagram.

6 Ask students to record the name of one concept above the left-hand circle and one above the right-hand circle.

7 Show students how to record differences between the two concepts on each circle and similarities in the overlapping portion of the circle.

Example

As part of a study of animals, fourth-grade teacher Jamie Yates involved her students in reading *A Whale Is Not a Fish and Other Animal Mix-Ups* by Melvin Berger (1996). This book contains a series of comparisons between different animals including donkeys and mules, porpoises and dolphins, and toads and frogs. After students had read the book, Jamie assigned students to work in pairs to create Venn Diagrams to reflect the animal comparisons detailed in the book. She distributed copies of the diagrams and assigned each pair a section of the text. Students then recorded the similarities and differences between their animals on the diagram. An example of a comparison of porpoises and dolphins is shown below:

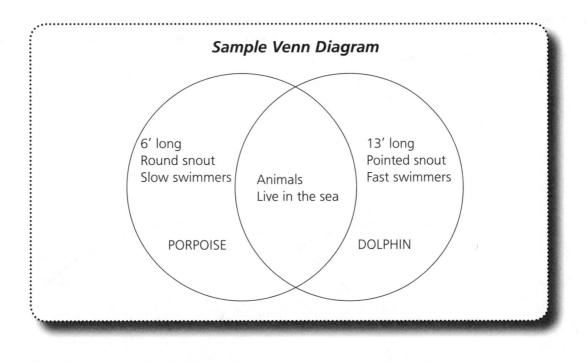

Sample Venn Diagram

6' long
Round snout
Slow swimmers

Animals
Live in the sea

13' long
Pointed snout
Fast swimmers

PORPOISE

DOLPHIN

References

Berger, M. (1996). *A whale is not a fish and other animal mix-ups.* New York: Scholastic.
(I).

Your Turn!

Select a book, section of a textbook, or magazine article that uses the comparison–contrast structure. Select a text from the appendix at the end of this book, or one of your own choosing. Introduce the concept of comparison–contrast and teach students the associated signal words. Then give students the Venn Diagram on the next page, explaining that it is a way to record similarities and differences in ideas. After students have finished reading, have them label each of the circles according to the concepts being compared. For example, if they are comparing bats and birds they should record the word *bats* above one circle and *birds* above the other. Then, show them how to record differences in each side of the circles and similarities in the overlapping section.

Venn Diagram

Directions: Think about the similarities and differences between the two topics you studied. Label each circle with the name of one of the topics. List the similarities where the circles overlap and the differences in each of the circles.

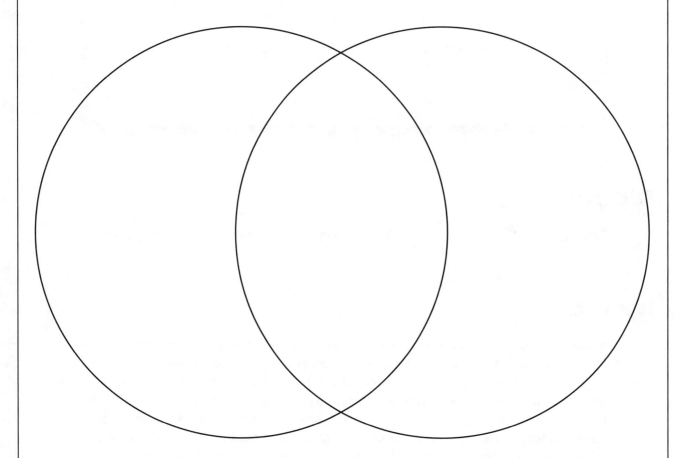

Cause–Effect Map

GRADE LEVELS: 3–12

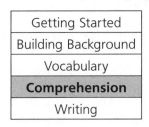

What Is It?

The cause–effect structure introduces a description of events and their causes. Words like *if, so, so that, because of, as a result of, since, in order to,* and *cause and effect* cue readers to the presence of this structure. Cause–Effect Maps provide a visual means of recording information reflecting this structure. Students often encounter cause and effect in science and social studies. The cause–effect structure is evident in materials for primary grade students as well as those for high school students.

What Is Its Purpose?

Cause–Effect Maps encourage students to analyze texts for the cause–effect structure. They focus students on not only identifying this structuring, but recording it on a visual organizer that helps them to see the structure in action.

What Do I Do?

1 Have students think–pair–share personal stories in which they can demonstrate cause and effect. For example, students could share how they were punished (effect) for staying out past curfew (cause).

2 Select an informational text related to your content area that presents a cause and effect.

3 Involve the students in the reading of the article, focusing on signal words. These signal words should be written on a chart for fast reference. (Using an overhead or document camera, model how you attend to signal words. Highlight or underline these signal words as you read.)

4 Distribute the Cause–Effect Map and explain the instructions.

5 Have students work in pairs to complete the map.

6 Review student responses. Have students present their Cause–Effect Map or grade individually. Make sure that the students can describe the relationship between cause and effect.

Example

High school health teacher David Downey was beginning a unit on drugs and their dangers. To help students understand this topic, he introduced the cause–effect structure using an article appearing on *Time.com* entitled "How Cocaine Scrambles Genes in the Brain" (*www.time.com/time/health/article/0,8599,1952411,00.html*). This article explained the effect of cocaine on the brain in terms of its impact on the way genes in the brain function. David began the lesson by getting students to identify examples of cause and effect in their everyday life. For example, because of tardiness, a student may be given demerits. He then asked students to reflect on what they already know about the effects of drugs on the body and mind.

At this point, David read to students some easy examples of cause–effect structures from newspapers and magazines. He introduced the idea of signal words and listed them on chart paper. He explained that authors do not always use signal words. He then asked students to listen for signal words as he read a passage aloud and used a think-aloud strategy to help students understand the thinking involved in identifying cause and effect.

Next, students read the article to themselves. After reading, they worked in groups to complete Cause–Effect Maps (see sample below). These maps consisted of one box at the top indicating the cause of the event, and several boxes underneath to indicate the various effects resulting from the cause. When they finished the students shared and explained their answers using the document camera. Students were encouraged to go back to the text to defend their answers. David also asked them to consider how the identified effects might turn into causes and what the consequences of these new causes might be.

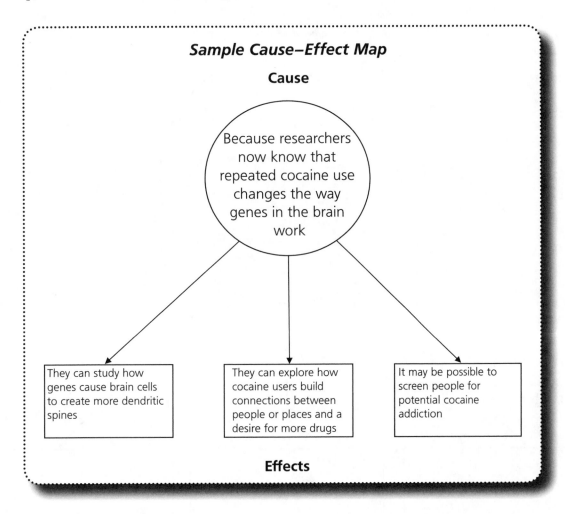

References

Slavavitz, M. (2010, January 8). How cocaine scrambles genes in the brain. *Time Magazine*. Retrieved from *www.time.com/time/health/article/0,8599,1952411,00.html*.

Your Turn!

Select a text with a clear cause–effect pattern from the appendix at the back of this book, or one of your own choosing. Introduce the idea of cause and effect with your students by relating it to real life in some way (*because* I lost my lunch money, I couldn't eat lunch). Remind students of the signal words associated with this structure. Introduce the Cause–Effect Map on the next page, and ask students to read to note the cause and the effect.

Cause–Effect Map

Directions: Record the cause that you noted in the reading in the circle. Then record the effects of that cause in the boxes beneath it.

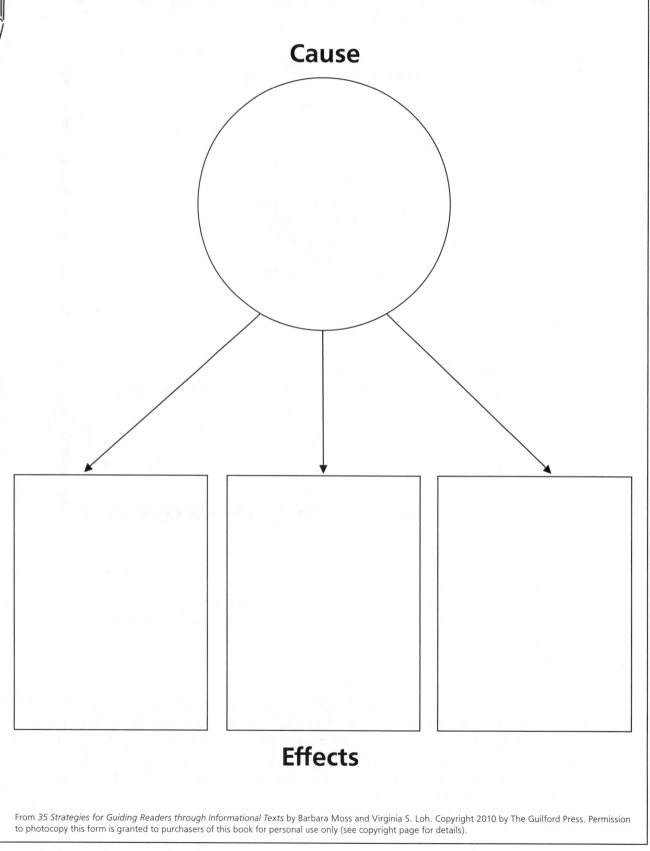

Cause

Effects

Problem Solution Outline

GRADE LEVELS: 3–12

Getting Started
Building Background
Vocabulary
Comprehension
Writing

What Is It?

The problem–solution expository text structure is one that students frequently encounter in content-area material. This structure is one that students need to understand if they are to successfully comprehend informational text. This text structure is signaled by words like *because, cause, since, as a result, so,* and *so that.*

What Is Its Purpose?

The Problem–Solution Outline is a visual organizer that focuses attention on passages that present a particular problem and a potential solution or solutions. This outline helps students focus on and record the nature of the problem and why it was a problem. It then requires students to consider attempted solutions to the problem, outcomes, and the end result.

What Do I Do?

1 Locate a text that illustrates the problem–solution pattern. Introduce the problem–solution pattern, reminding students to look for the signal words mentioned above.

2 Introduce the Problem–Solution Outline visual organizer, explaining that it provides for identification of who has the problem, what it is, and why it exists. It also requires that students identify attempted solutions and outcomes.

3 Ask students to read the passage with the purpose of identifying the problem, solution, and outcomes.

4 Have students work in pairs to identify the pattern in the text and complete the Problem–Solution Outline.

Example

Teacher Andrea Jackson involved her American history students in the study of the California gold rush. They read Rhoda Blumberg's (1989) *The Great American Gold Rush* as part of this study. To help sensitize the students to the critical dangers of fire in San Francisco at this time, she introduced the problem–solution structure. She showed the students several examples of texts illustrating this structure. Andrea highlighted the signal words typically used with problem–solution. She then asked the students to read a brief section about some of the problems that plagued the early city of San Francisco described in Blumberg's book. After their reading, she introduced the Problem–Solution Outline. Andrea explained the organizer and the class worked as a group to complete the outline shown below:

Sample Problem Solution Outline

Problem	
Who has the problem?	*The city of San Francisco.*
What was the problem?	*Fires were commonplace.*
Why was it a problem?	*Most buildings were made of wood and burned easily.*

Solution	Outcome
City dwellers and businessmen started to build buildings out of bricks.	*Buildings were more resistant to fire.*

End Result
Rebuilding was no longer necessary after every fire because the new buildings were fire resistant.

References

Blumberg, R. (1989). *The great American gold rush*. New York: Atheneum. (M).

Your Turn!

Select a text from the appendix at the back of the book, or one of your own choosing. Ask students to read the text, looking for signal words associated with this structure and the problem and solution described in the text. After that, involve students in completing the organizer on the next page.

Problem–Solution Organizer

Directions: Think of the problem and solution you read about. Record information about the problem, solution, outcome, and end result in the boxes below.

Problem

Who has the problem?

What was the problem?

Why was it a problem?

Solution	Outcome

End Result

PART FIVE

Writing
Strategies

I Remember

GRADE LEVELS: K–5

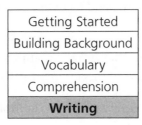

Getting Started
Building Background
Vocabulary
Comprehension
Writing

What Is It?

I Remember (Hoyt, 2009) helps to focus students on the content of informational text at the same time it provides young children with an opportunity to express themselves in writing. I Remember is typically used during a teacher read-aloud of an informational text, but can also be adapted for use when students are reading this text type independently. The teacher reads a small section of text aloud, and at a logical stopping point, students stop to think about what they remember about the text. They then share this information with the group, initially through speaking, and later through writing.

What Is Its Purpose?

I Remember is an excellent strategy for developing students' listening and oral language skills when working with informational texts. It requires students to listen to gather information and then produce language focused on that information. Once students are able to express the information orally, they are then ready to respond to informational text through writing.

What Do I Do?

1 Select an informational book for reading aloud to your students. The book should be appropriate to their age and abilities.

2 Break the reading into small chunks of text by identifying stopping points.

3 Write the sentence stem "I remember" on a sentence strip.

4 Prepare students for listening to the text by having them predict the book content from the cover (see Strategy 8). You may also want to introduce new vocabulary words.

5 Remind students that they need to listen and remember. Read a small section of the text aloud.

6 Model for students how they might complete the sentence stem "I remember" orally by completing the stem with pertinent information from the text.

7 Continue reading by asking students to complete the stem orally at various stopping points.

8 Model for students how to record their oral responses in writing by completing the I Remember Chart. Have them work with a partner to first state their responses orally and then record them in writing.

Example

Teacher Hilary Sanchez's first graders enjoy studying informational trade books. Hilary regularly reads these books aloud to her students. To help them develop their listening skills, Hilary decided to teach her students the I Remember strategy.

Hilary began the lesson by explaining to the students that they would be working on remembering what they hear. She reminded them that they needed to think while she was reading in order to remember facts from the book she had chosen. She showed them a chart with the words "I remember that _____" written in large print, and reminded students that they would use these words to start their sentences.

Hilary introduced the read-aloud of *Ladybugs: Red, Fiery and Bright* (Posada, 2002) by showing students the pictures in the text and getting them to predict what some of the information in the book might be. At this point she explained to students that she would read the book aloud to them and stop periodically to give them a chance to remember information from the text.

Hilary put the text on the document camera and read the first two pages aloud to the students. At this point she stopped and modeled for students how to create a sentence starting with "I remember that." She pointed to the words on the chart and said "I remember that ladybugs have black spots and red backs." She recorded this statement on the chart so that students could see it. She then invited students to contribute their own "I remember" statements. Several students gave answers, and Hilary recorded these on the chart. Sample responses are recorded below:

Sample I Remember Responses

I remember that ___*ladybugs lay eggs.*___

I remember that ___*ladybugs control aphids.*___

I remember that ___*ladybugs molt.*___

She continued reading the book, stopping at strategic points. She continued to follow this pattern of modeling statements for students and then recording their responses on the chart.

At this point Hilary distributed copies of the last two pages of the text to the students. She read the text aloud to them, and then asked each student to think of an "I remember" statement. She then had students share their statements with a partner orally and then record them in writing. She circulated around the room monitoring their responses.

References

Hoyt, L. (2009). *Revisit, reflect, retell: Time-tested strategies for teaching reading comprehension* (updated ed.). Portsmouth, NH: Heinemann.

Posada, M. (2002). *Ladybugs: Red, fiery and bright.* New York: Carolrhoda. (P).

Your Turn!

Select an informational text to read aloud to your students or have them read independently. Select a text from the appendix at the end of this book, or one of your own choosing. Model the I Remember strategy for them, and then have them practice making "I remember" statements orally at strategic points in the text. As students become more skilled with the strategy, they can write or draw what they remember in the spaces provided on the template.

I Remember Chart

Directions: Work with a partner to write down three things you remember from the book.

I remember that _____.

I remember that _____.

I remember that _____.

Written Retellings

GRADE LEVELS: 2–12

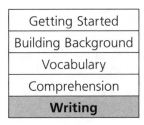

Getting Started
Building Background
Vocabulary
Comprehension
Writing

What Is It?

Written Retellings require students to recount what they recall after reading or hearing a text, either orally or in writing. Written Retellings give teachers insights into students' abilities to interact with, explore, and draw conclusions from a text. Written Retellings are an excellent way to improve student comprehension of expository text. Most teachers are aware of the ways that narrative retellings can improve text understanding; expository retellings can be equally useful in this area.

What Is Its Purpose?

Both Oral and Written Retellings let students play an active role in reconstructing text and require students to restructure materials they have read into their own form, a process requiring clear understanding of text content. Written Retellings also provide teachers with an excellent means of assessment, allowing them to see *how* as well as *how much* information students retain after reading or listening to a text. Informational text retellings also give teachers insights about students' sensitivity to genre and their ability to organize information. Written Retellings can engage students in reflecting on their thoughts about the connections between their own lives and the informational trade books they are reading.

Student of all ages can benefit from Oral Retellings of expository text. Students in grades 3 and up are most likely to benefit from Written Retellings, though some younger student may have success with this strategy as well. Teachers can track students' writing fluency through retellings and evaluate their understanding of informational texts. This strategy can also be useful with struggling middle grade and secondary readers, or with English language learners. English language learners may benefit particularly from this strategy, since the concrete nature of informational text can help them build bridges between their first and second languages. Linguistic matches may be more obvious when objects or animals are the focus of learning.

What Do I Do?

A three-phase sequence may facilitate student development of skills in Written Retelling. First, students can do retellings based on listening to short read-alouds of informational picture books or brief magazine or newspaper articles. After that, students can read texts appropriate to their level on their own and retell. Later, students can move into listening or reading texts and creating Written Retellings.

The following steps can guide the process:

1 Prior to reading a text aloud, teachers should help students begin to think about the content of the book through strategies such as KWHL (Strategy 6). They might use the prediction questions in the Shared Reading (Strategy 4) lesson as a guide. After reading a text aloud, the teacher might "think aloud" as he or she retells and/or asks students to evaluate the retelling to see whether the teacher missed any important parts.

2 Students should practice retelling in pairs or small groups after listening to a text. Teachers can guide students during this phase, encouraging them to note text organizations and structures. During this phase, teachers might involve students in completing graphic organizers reflective of these structures.

3 As students become more skilled in retelling materials read orally, they can begin to engage in Written Retellings. Brown, Bransford, Ferrara, and Campione (1983) recommend the following steps for involving students in Written Retellings of expository text:

  ◆ First, for several days prior to retelling, students should be immersed in a study of the topic of the text that will be retold. This can involve shared book experiences (Strategy 4), informational text read-alouds (Strategy 3), sustained silent reading, and/or brainstorming of information learned.

  ◆ Second, the teacher distributes the text to be retold, folded so that only the title is visible.

  ◆ Next, students write a sentence or two indicating what they think the text will be about (Strategy 8). They then predict words that might be found in the selection. Following this, they share their predictions with one another.

- At this point, the teacher reads the text aloud as students follow along. Students reread the text as many times as they wish, jotting notes or creating visual organizers (see Strategies 20–25). They then write their retellings.

- After writing their retellings, students share their retellings with one another. They compare their work, discussing similarities and differences. They can also evaluate their retellings using a checklist or a rubric like the one on the next page.

Example

First-grade teacher Diane James decided to begin involving her students in Written Retellings in order to familiarize them with the nature of expository text. She began by reading simple books aloud, sometimes several times, and engaged her students in group Oral Retellings of the text. She had also modeled how to create a Written Retelling.

Toward the end of the year, Diane planned a read-aloud of Millicent Selsam's (1992) *How Kittens Grow*. She asked students to write sentences explaining what they thought the book would be about and predict words they might hear. She then read the book aloud as students followed along. She then cut apart several copies of the text, and mounted key photographs demonstrating the book's sequence of events (Strategy 24) on cardboard. Children worked in pairs to sequence the pictures. They then retold the events of the book to one another. At this point, they used sentence frames (Strategy 33) provided by Diane to work in pairs to retell the text in writing (see sample below). They provided each other with feedback on the quality of their retellings using the Informational Text Retelling Form as a guide. After that, Diane reread the book aloud. At this point, the students discussed the sections of texts that they missed during their retellings and added to their Written Retellings.

Sample Written Retelling

The title of the book is _How Kittens Grow_. It is written by _Millicent E. Selsam_. The book starts out when _a mother cat has just given birth to four kittens. The kittens' eyes and ears are closed. The kittens suck milk from their mother_. When the kittens are 2 weeks old _they open their eyes and weigh twice as much as when they were born_. When the kittens are 4 weeks old _they can go over to the mother to nurse and can see and hear and play_. When the kittens are 5 weeks old _they drink from a saucer and learn to eat solid food and hunt_. When they are 8 weeks old _they eat solid food, hunt, and run. They can do everything an adult kitten does. This is when you should get a kitten._

References

Brown, A. L., Bransford, J. W., Ferrara, R. F., & Campione, J. (1983). Learning, remembering, and understanding. In J. Flavell & E. Markham (Eds.), *Handbook of child psychology* (pp. 393–451). New York: Wiley.

Selsam, M. (1992). *How kittens grow.* New York: Four Winds Press. (P).

Your Turn!

Try using a Written Retelling with your students. Use prereading activities to get them ready to listen to a book you read aloud. Then have them listen to you read a simple expository text. Then put students in pairs to retell orally. After that, let them record what they have written to create a Written Retelling. After the students have created their Written Retelling, hand out the forms on the next page. Have each student evaluate the other student's Written Retelling of the book, using the simple checklist to evaluate their partner's performance.

Informational Text Retelling Form

Directions: Complete the form below.

Name _____ **Book Used** _____

1　Make a check mark next to the things your partner did well.

_____ **Mentioned the author and title of the book**

_____ **Remembered and included the main ideas**

_____ **Remembered the details**

_____ **Put the information in the right order**

_____ **Gave accurate information**

_____ **Knew how the text was organized**

_____ **Used the vocabulary words found in the book**

_____ **Wrote in complete sentences**

2　Using the space below, write about how you think your partner did. What could he or she do better next time?

_____

_____

_____

_____

_____

_____

_____

Readers' Theatre

GRADE LEVELS: 2–12

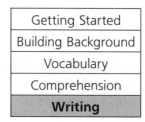

| Getting Started |
| Building Background |
| Vocabulary |
| Comprehension |
| **Writing** |

What Is It?

Readers' Theatre is the oral presentation of text by a group of readers. Readers' Theatre does not typically include props, costumes, or memorization of lines, which makes it an ideal strategy to use for many students. Students must, however, read their parts fluently, with appropriate dramatic flair and proper intonation. Readers' Theatre is often used with folktales or narrative texts, but can be easily adapted to informational texts.

What Is Its Purpose?

The purpose of Readers' Theatre is to give students the opportunity to engage in a dramatic presentation of a text. Another critical purpose of Readers' Theatre is to develop reading fluency. Readers' Theatre can help students visualize the action in a story in ways that simply reading a text cannot. It can provide a means for improving student comprehension of a text in a motivating, engaging format.

Informational books and biographies with dialogue are easily adapted to this format, but picture books or excerpts from longer books can also be effective. Informational trade books like King and Osborne's (1997) *Oh Freedom!: Kids Talk about the Civil Rights Movement with the People Who Made It Happen* or *Owen and*

Mzee: The True Story of a Remarkable Friendship (Hatkoff, Hatkoff, & Kahumbu, 2006) are excellent examples of books that can be easily adapted to this format.

What Do I Do?

The following guidelines can help teachers adapt informational texts to a Readers' Theatre Script (Young & Vardell, 1993):

1 Choose an interesting section of text containing the desired content.

2 Reproduce the text.

3 Delete lines not critical to the content being emphasized, including those indicating that a character is speaking. The narrator's role is often important in informational texts.

4 Decide how to divide the parts for the readers. Dialogue can be assigned to appropriate characters. With some texts, it will be necessary to rewrite text as dialogue or with multiple narrators. Changing the third-person point of view to the first-person point of view ("I" or "we") can create effective narration.

5 Add a prologue to introduce the script in storylike fashion. If needed, a postscript can be added to bring closure to the script.

6 Label the readers' parts by placing the speaker's name in the left-hand margin, followed by a colon.

7 When the script is finished, ask others to read it aloud. Listening to the script may make it easier to make appropriate revisions.

8 Give students time to read and rehearse their parts.

An obvious next step for using Reader's Theatre is to involve students in selecting books from which they can develop their own Readers' Theatre Script. Through this activity, learners develop critical thinking skills, make decisions, work cooperatively, and engage in the process of revision.

Example

Third-grade teacher Kelly Evans decided to involve her students in using a Readers' Theatre Script she developed based on *Abe's Honest Words: The Life of Abraham Lincoln* (Rappaport, 2008). She introduced the script using a KWHL (Strategy 6) and involved her students in reading the script as a group. After her students read the script and discussed it, she assigned each student a part. At this point, the students formed pairs and practiced their parts using paired reading. After each student had ample time to practice, the students worked as a class to read the entire script. After several experiences with different scripts, Kelly began to involve her students in creating their own scripts based on some of the books recommended above. She modeled the writing of a Readers' Theatre Script and then divided students into teams to create their own.

References

Hatkoff, I., Hatkoff, C., & Kahumbu, P. (2006). *Owen and Mzee: The true story of remarkable friendship.* New York: Scholastic. (P).

King, C., & Osborne, L. B. (1997). *Oh freedom!: Kids talk about the civil rights movement with the people who made it happen.* New York: Knopf. (YA).

Rappaport, D. (2008). *Abe's honest words: The life of Abraham Lincoln.* New York: Hyperion. (P).

Young, T. A., & Vardell, S. M. (1993). Weaving reader's theatre and nonfiction into the curriculum. *The Reading Teacher, 46,* 396–406.

Your Turn!

Pick one of the books suggested and develop a Readers' Theatre script around it. Follow the steps outlined above, or, for more information, consult Young and Vardell's (1993) article listed in the references. After students have experience in doing Readers' Theatre, they may wish to write their own scripts. The handout on the next page provides a "first step" in this process. Students can record the speaker's name on the short line on the left, and what the person will say on the lines on the right.

Readers' Theatre Script

Directions: Think about how you will turn your book into a script. Who will the speakers be? What will each person say? Record the names of the speakers on the short lines and the words they will say on the longer lines.

Speakers: _____

_____

_____

_____: _____

_____

_____

_____: _____

_____

_____

_____: _____

_____

_____

_____: _____

_____

_____

_____: _____

_____

_____

········· **Strategy 31** ·················

Two-Column Journal

GRADE LEVELS: K–5

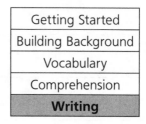

| Getting Started |
| Building Background |
| Vocabulary |
| Comprehension |
| **Writing** |

What Is It?

Two-Column Journals let students record and respond to expository text, promoting both aesthetic or emotional and efferent or factual responses to literature. On one side of a Two-Column Journal, students record facts found in a book, magazine, or newspaper article. They record words or phrases directly from the text or restate text information in their own words. On the right side of the journal, they describe their feelings or emotional responses to those facts.

What Is Its Purpose?

The purpose of the Two-Column Journal is to get students to think about their learning more deeply through the act of writing. By reflecting on what they think about what they learn, students are reminded of the need to be actively engaged in their reading, and to make connections between the text itself and their own lives.

What Do I Do?

1 Select an appropriate book, magazine, or newspaper article.

2 Have students divide a piece of paper in half, folding vertically.

3 On the left side of the paper, have students write "What It Said" on the top line.

4 On the right side of the paper, have students write "What I Thought" on the top line.

5 Ask students to identify a specified number of interesting facts from the reading material. Have them record each fact on the left side of the paper. Next to each fact, have students record their reactions or feelings about each fact on the right side of the paper.

6 Discuss their facts and reactions in the large group.

Example

Fifth-grade teacher Colin Danes involved his students in a unit of study on immigration. As part of that study, his students read *Immigrant Kids* (Freedman, 1995). After they completed their reading, Colin asked the students to complete Two-Column Journals related to the book. He instructed students to identify four facts they learned from the book and record them on the left side of their Two-Column Journals under "What It Said." They were also instructed to record their reaction to each fact, or "What I Thought," on the right side (see an example of one student's work below). After completing their journals, students shared them in small groups, discussing their facts and their responses.

Sample: Two Column Journal

What It Said	What I Thought
1. Children back then had to work to support their families.	1. I don't think kids should have to work to support their families.
2. Children back then were interested in baseball.	2. I love baseball too, just like the kids back then.
3. Kids back then formed gangs that fought with sticks and stones.	3. Kids today sometimes form gangs, but they fight with guns.
4. Immigrant kids back then had to memorize facts in school.	4. Kids today still have to memorize in school, so I guess schools haven't changed that much.

References

Freedman, R. (1995). *Immigrant kids*. New York: Puffin. (I).

Your Turn!

Select a book, magazine, or newspaper article for your students to read. Select a text from the appendix at the end of this book, or one of your own choosing. After students have read, have them record four or five facts about what they have read under "What It Said" and their reactions to those facts under "What I Thought." The sheet on the next page provides a template for their answers.

Two-Column Journal

Directions: Write down what the book said in the column on the left. For each statement, write down what you thought or felt about it.

What It Said	What I Thought

Learning Log

GRADE LEVELS: 3–12

Getting Started
Building Background
Vocabulary
Comprehension
Writing

What Is It?

Learning Logs are notebooks in which students record information about content-related material. This information can include questions, drawings, webs, charts, and so on (Bromley, 1993). Learning Logs do not involve formal writing experiences, but emphasize using writing as a reflective task designed to facilitate information retrieval.

What Is Its Purpose?

Learning Logs allow students to record information about learning using the format of their choice: diagram, drawing, illustration, or text. This strategy provides the student with a record of his or her learning over time, which can be helpful when reviewing for tests or quizzes.

What Do I Do?

1 To involve students in using Learning Logs, teachers should require them to purchase spiral-bound notebooks or bound composition books to be designated as a Learning Log.

2 Select content-area material appropriate to the students' abilities.

3 Model the various types of Learning Log activities that students can use to respond to text. These experiences can occur before, during, or after reading. They can include requiring students to write predictions about the content (Strategy 8), do quickwrites, create Data Charts (Strategy 21), develop webs (Strategy 20), or use illustrations to remember key pieces of information.

4 Assign Learning Log activities. These activities can be shared in small groups. Direct students to review their Learning Log writings in preparation for tests, group presentations, or other classroom-related activities.

Example

Sixth-grade science teacher Wade Duram involved his students in small readings of a variety of texts about weather. After reading every two chapters, students were required to record information learned in their Learning Logs. They had the option of drawing, doing quickwrites, or recording webs in their logs. After reading *Hurricanes: Earth's Mightiest Storms* (Lauber, 2001), one student recorded the following illustration in his learning log. This visual depicts the process whereby a hurricane develops.

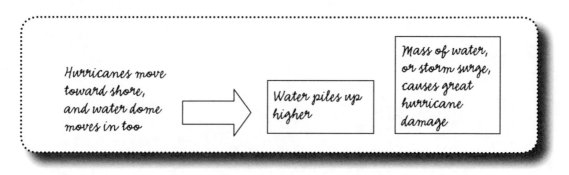

References

Bromley, K. (1993). *Journaling: Engagements in reading, writing, and thinking.* New York: Scholastic.

Lauber, P. (2001). *Hurricanes: Earth's mightiest storms.* New York: Houghton Mifflin Press. (M).

Your Turn!

A template for a Learning Log appears on the next page. Using an expository text, involve students in recording information in their Learning Logs. Select a text from the appendix at the end of this book, or one of your own choosing. First, show students samples of some of the different ways they can record information in their logs, such as diagrams, quickwrites, vocabulary, and/or webs. Then give them the opportunity to record information on the template.

Learning Log

TOPIC: _____

New Vocabulary That I Learned:

Word	Definition	Picture/Sentence

Ideas That I Need to Remember:

Record important information from the text here. You can use webs, quickwrites, or pictures to help you remember the information.

· **Strategy 33** ·

Paragraph Writing Frame

GRADE LEVELS: 2–12

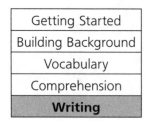

| Getting Started |
| Building Background |
| Vocabulary |
| Comprehension |
| **Writing** |

What Is It?

Paragraph Writing Frames are an excellent way to scaffold student writing of expository text (Armbruster, Anderson, & Ostertag, 1989). They are equally effective with young children or older children who struggle with writing. Originally designed for use with textbook material, they are equally useful with informational trade books and magazine or newspaper articles. These frames help students to further their understanding of the most frequently encountered expository text patterns, which include description, sequence, comparison–contrast, cause–effect, and problem–solution.

Paragraph Writing Frames employ the cloze procedure, providing sentence starters that include signal words or phrases. When these are completed, students have written a paragraph that follows one of the most commonly used expository text structures. They provide an excellent follow up to strategies presented earlier in this text, such as Semantic Map (Strategy 23), Series of Events Chart (Strategy 24), Venn Diagram (Strategy 25), Cause–Effect Map (Strategy 26), and Problem–Solution Outline (Strategy 27). After learning about each expository text pattern through these strategies, students can then try their hand at writing paragraphs illustrating each pattern.

What Is Its Purpose?

These frames help students to further their understanding of the most frequently encountered expository text patterns, which include description, sequence, comparison–contrast, cause–effect, and problem–solution. They effectively scaffold students' efforts to use these structures in their own writing.

What Do I Do?

1 Introduce the various frames one at a time. First, model the writing of a sample paragraph illustrating the organizational pattern being introduced. For example, the teacher could write a paragraph about a topic that illustrates sequence. In this paragraph, he or she would use signal words like *first*, *next*, *then*, and *finally*.

2 After that, the teacher would review the sequence of events in the paragraph and with the group.

3 At this point, the teacher would give students the sentences on sentence strips and have them arrange the sentences in order.

4 Depending on their ability, students might then copy the strips in paragraph form onto their papers.

5 The teacher then introduces Paragraph Writing Frames to the large group and fills them in with the students' responses. It may be helpful for students to have the first sentence of the frame provided for them.

Example

Teacher Jane Hammond worked with seventh-grade English language learners. Writing was a real struggle for these students. Jane had been working to help these students recognize the various expository text structures for some time. It was now time to involve them in writing about these structures. Jane decided to use the comparison–contrast structure for her focus. She showed the students a written sample of work illustrating the comparison–contrast pattern. She helped them to identify the signal words in the passage. She then introduced the Paragraph Writing Frame, explaining to students that it was similar to the cloze strategy they had used before. At this point, Jane read aloud a section from *George vs. George: The American Revolution as Seen from Both Sides* (Schanzer, 2007), an excellent trade book that explores the American Revolution from the points of view of George Washington and George III. She read aloud the part of the text that compared life in England with life in the colonies.

At this point, students completed a comparison–contrast frame as illustrated below. The students' words are italicized in the example.

> Life in England and in the colonies were different in many ways. First, *many people in England lived in London, Europe's largest city, but most colonists lived on farms.* Second, *England's wealthy city dwellers spent time in city-based coffeehouses, taverns, and gardens, while most colonists were middle class and included farmers, shopkeepers, teachers, and craftsmen.* Third, *British cities were polluted with smog, while American towns had beautiful forests, fish, and game.* Finally, *the poor in England included beggars and pickpockets while poor colonists were usually laborers, indentured servants, and slaves.*

References

Armbruster, B., Anderson, T. H., & Ostertag, J. (1989). Teaching text structure to improve reading and writing. *The Reading Teacher, 43,* 130–137.

Schanzer, R. (2007). *George vs. George: The American revolution as seen from both sides.* Washington, DC: National Geographic. (I).

Your Turn!

Introduce your students to writing expository text frames using the suggestions outlined above. Then have them try out the frames found on the next page. You may wish to modify these, depending on the subject and topic being studied.

Paragraph Writing Frames

Description Frame

_____ have many interesting

features. First, they have _____, which

allow them to _____. Second, they

have _____, which are _____

_____.

Last, they have _____

_____, which

_____

_____.

Sequence Frame

The first step in making a _____ is to

_____.

After that, you must _____

_____.

Third, you need to _____

_____.

Finally, you _____

_____.

(cont.)

Comparison Frame

_____ are alike in many ways.

First, both are _____ and

_____. Second, they have similar

_____. Finally, they both

_____.

Contrast Frame

_____ were different in many

ways. First, they differed because _____,

while _____. A second difference was

that _____.

A third difference was _____.

Finally, another difference was _____.

Cause–Effect Frame

Because of _____,

_____

happened. Therefore, _____.

This explains why _____.

Problem–Solution Frame

The problem was that _____.

This problem happened because _____.

The problem was finally solved when _____.

I Used to Think …
but Now I Know …

GRADE LEVELS: 2–12

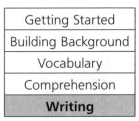

| Getting Started |
| Building Background |
| Vocabulary |
| Comprehension |
| **Writing** |

What Is It?

I Used to Think … but Now I Know … (Koch, 1990) is a poetic sentence frame that can be used to teach any content area. It provides a clear structure that students can use to state their preconceptions about a topic. Through the reading of informational texts, students will develop the abilities to question this preconception and to refer to the text for confirmation or to replace it with fact.

This strategy is also a way to combine poetry and informational texts. These two genres are generally thought of as being opposites, since poetry typically elicits aesthetic, or feeling-type responses, while informational texts elicit more efferent, or factual-type responses (Rosenblatt, 2004). By completing a series of I Used to Think … but Now I Know … frames, students can create a poem about an informational text.

What Is Its Purpose?

The purposes of the I Used to Think … but Now I Know … sentence frames are to enhance students' appreciation for poetry, to access their prior knowledge, and to measure what students have learned from a particular text or unit of study. In addition, this strategy allows students an opportunity to critically think about their conceptions as the idea is to refute or change current thinking.

What Do I Do?

This strategy is best used before and after reading an informational text or at the beginning and end of a unit of study in accompaniment with KWHL (Strategy 6).

1 Model the strategy. For example, in introducing a unit of the American Revolution, you could think aloud the following (adopted from Koch, 1990):

- ◆ I USED TO THINK   *that there were fifteen colonies,*
- ◆ BUT NOW I KNOW   *there were thirteen original colonies.*
- ◆ I USED TO THINK   *the Americans and British were the only countries fighting in the war,*
- ◆ BUT NOW I KNOW   *the French were our allies and helped American colonists win.*

2 Begin a class discussion about the topic of study. Have students share what they think they know about the topic.

3 Have students write some of their preconceptions following the sentence frame "I used to think.... " Have the students write six to nine of them as some frames may not be used if they are true. For example, a student could write "I used to think *that George Washington was a general in the Revolutionary War....* " This sentence would be true so there would be no need to finish the frame. This student would eliminate this particular frame from his or her poem.

4 Select an informational text about the topic under study. The topic should be one about which students have limited prior knowledge.

5 Read aloud the text. Set a purpose for reading by telling the students to listen to hear whether their "facts" are correct or whether they need to be changed.

6 For younger groups, you might want to scaffold and list some facts learned from the story onto chart paper. Students can refer to this collection of learned facts to confirm their preconceptions or refute their misconceptions.

7 Have students complete the "But now I know ... " sentence frame with the appropriate fact.

8 Have students share their poems with a partner.

9 Optional: For the sentences that were correct, instead of eliminating them, the students could change their frames to "I used to think ... AND now I know that I was right!" This might be a good opportunity to explicitly teach the students on the use of the conjunctions *and* versus *but*.

Example

Ms. Marilyn Ware is an eighth-grade science teacher. As part of the science standards, she taught a unit on the chemistry of living things. Before starting the unit, she did a KWHL (Strategy 6) with her students. After completing the KWH sections as a whole group, she paired up the students. (Since Ms. Ware teaches in a school with a large population of English language learners, she made sure to partner a proficient or native speaker with a beginning to intermediate speaker.)

Ms. Wave wrote the following vocabulary words and concepts on the board: *cell, mitochondria, DNA, RNA, ribosomes,* and *enzymes.* She had each pair talk about what they thought each of the six terms meant; each pair were instructed to complete the sentence frame "We used to think … " (They left the "But now we know … " sentence frame blank at this point.)

Then, Ms. Wave used the document camera with a read-aloud from an informational trade book. She read the first chapter on "Building Blocks" from *Biology: Life as We Know It* by Dan Green (2008). As she read, she had the pairs complete their sentence frames: "But now we know.… " For example, one pair came up with "We used to think *that mitochondria was something that plants produced,* but now we know *that mitochondria are like power plants working inside cells to burn food in order to make ATP or energy.*"

Ms. Wave gave each pair a large piece of poster paper and had them record their sentence frames on the paper along with appropriate illustrations. The next day, she hung the posters up around the room and to review, she had the students walk around and read each poster; this particular strategy is often referred to as a Gallery Walk.

References

Green, D. (2008). *Biology: Life as we know it.* New York: Kingfisher. (YA).

Koch, K. (1990). *Rose, where did you get that red?: Teaching great poetry to children.* New York: Vintage.

Rosenblatt, L. (2004). The transactional theory of reading and writing. In R. B. Ruddell & N. J. Unrau (Eds.), *Theoretical models and processes of reading* (5th ed., pp. 1363–1398). Newark, DE: International Reading Association.

Your Turn!

Select an informational trade book addressing your topic from the appendix at the back of this book or one of your own choosing. This strategy works best when your students have a limited knowledge base about the subject. Distribute the following worksheet and model an example.

Writing Strategies

"I Used to Think ... but Now I Know ..." Sentence Frames

Directions: Complete each frame by telling what you used to think and what you think now.

Topic: _____

I used to think _____

but now I know _____.

I used to think _____

but now I know _____.

I used to think _____

but now I know _____.

I used to think _____

but now I know _____.

I used to think _____

but now I know _____.

Summary Writing

GRADE LEVELS: 3–12

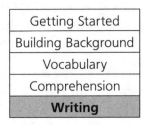

| Getting Started |
| Building Background |
| Vocabulary |
| Comprehension |
| **Writing** |

What Is It?

Summary writing (adapted from Klinger & Vaughn, 1998) involves distilling information to its most essential components. A good summary uses as few words as possible to provide a brief overview of the content of a text or section on a text. Effective summaries include only the main ideas from a text; they do not include extraneous details. Summary Writing is an essential skill for school and workplace success. It can be used at any grade level from third through high school. Writing informational text summaries demands some different skills from summarizing a narrative, since it often involves the ability to use appropriate vocabulary terms and key concepts rather than story events.

What Is Its Purpose?

The purpose of Summary Writing is to provide a brief overview of a longer piece of work. The ability to summarize in writing requires students to analyze and synthesize information and to look beyond details to big ideas in a text. Students who can capably summarize texts demonstrate deep understanding of the most important ideas in a text.

What Do I Do?

1 Present an informational text to your students. Select a text that students are already familiar with.

2 Explain to students that it is often easier to know the main points from a text than to have to remember all of the details. When you write a summary, you have a record of the most important points from a text.

3 Show students a sample of a summary of a text they have read earlier. Point out to them that the summary is short, contains only the main points from the text, and condenses these points into very few words.

4 Explain to students that a main idea consists of two component parts: the who or what and the most important information about the who or what. To create a summary students must combine these components into a sentence of no more than 20 words.

5 Read aloud the first paragraph of the text. Think aloud as you identify the who or what and the most important information about the who or what. Record this information on the board. Then show students how to combine this information into a statement of no more than 20 words. Record this statement on the board.

6 Continue with this procedure for the rest of the text. Then show students how to combine each statement into a summary statement of no more than 20 words.

7 Then ask students to work with a partner to read a short text. Have them stop at specific points to complete the chart below as they think about the required information and condense it into a limited number of words. Then give them time to create a 20-word statement for their final summary of the book.

Example

Third-grade teacher Molly Bernstein's students were studying a unit on mammals. In order to teach her students about animal life cycles and how to summarize information, she decided to use the National Geographic book *Giant Pandas* (Reeder, 2005). Molly began the lesson by reviewing with students what they know about mammals. She then asked them what they know about pandas and why they are mammals.

Molly began the lesson on summarizing by showing students the section of the book on panda life cycles. She showed the book on the document camera and read aloud the first section of the text entitled "Birth." She thought aloud as she noted what the section was about and what was important about the birth of pandas. She recorded this on the Summary Writing Chart (see below). At this point, she created a 20-word summary of the information and recorded it on the chart. She then had students complete the last two sections, "Growth" and "Reproduction," with a partner, following the same format (see sample below). They summarized these two sections at the bottom of the chart.

Sample Summary Writing Chart

Title of the Book _Pandas_	Author _Tracey Reeder_
What was the title of this section? _Growth_	What was the title of this section? _Reproduction_
Who or what was this section about? _How pandas grow up and what they do_	Who or what was this section about? _How pandas get babies_
What was the important information about who or what this was about? • _Cubs can see at 6–8 weeks old._ • _Walks at 12 weeks_ • _8–9 months stops drinking milk and eats bamboo_ • _Lives on its own at 18 months_ • _Adult at 4–6 years_	What was the important information about who or what this was about? • _The female egg and male sperm come together._ • _The egg is fertilized._ • _A new baby grows in the mother's body._ • _After 160 days the baby is born._
Write a main idea sentence of no more than 20 words. _Pandas see at 6 weeks, walk at 12 weeks, eat bamboo at 8 months, and become adults at 4 years._	Write a main idea sentence of no more than 20 words. _Pandas reproduce when an egg and sperm join. Babies grow in the mother's body and are born after 160 days._

Now combine your main idea sentences to create a summary of no more than 20 words for the entire text.
Baby pandas grow up and become adults at 4 years. They then reproduce and babies are born after 160 days.

References

Klinger, J. K., & Vaughn, S. (1998). Using collaborative strategic reading. *Teaching Exceptional Children, 30*(6), 32–37.

Reeder, T. (2005). *Giant pandas*. Washington, DC: National Geographic. (I).

Your Turn!

Provide your students with an informational text. Select a text from the appendix at the end of this book, or one of your own choosing. After you model Summary Writing, have the students use the firm on the next page to summarize key sections and then combine those summaries for the section at the bottom.

Summary Writing Chart

Title of Book _____

Author _____

What was the title of this section? _____

Who or what was this section about? _____

What was the important information about who or what this was about?

- _____
- _____
- _____
- _____
- _____

Write a main idea sentence of no more than 20 words.

_____
_____
_____
_____

Now combine your main idea sentences to create a summary of no more than 20 words for the entire text.

_____
_____
_____
_____

Appendix

Recommended Materials

Quality Informational Trade Books

(P), primary grades 1–3; (I), intermediate grades 4–6; (M), middle grades 7–9; (YA) young adult grades 9–12.

Primary Books (Grades 1–3)

Aliki. (1996). *My visit to the aquarium.* New York: HarperCollins.

Aliki. (1999). *Communication.* New York: Greenwillow Books.

Ancona, G. (1994). *The piñata maker = El piñatero.* New York: Harcourt Brace.

Arnold, C. (1999). *South American animals.* New York: Morrow.

Arnosky, J. (2008). *All about alligators.* New York: Scholastic.

Aston, D. H. (2006). *An egg is quiet.* New York: Chronicle Books.

Aston, D. H. (2007). *A seed is sleepy.* New York: Chronicle Books.

Auch, A. (2002). *Tame and wild.* Minneapolis, MN: Compass Point Books.

Baer, E. (1992). *This is the way we go to school: A book about children around the world* (S. Bjorkman, Illus.). New York: Scholastic.

Bare, C. S. (1994). *Never kiss an alligator!* New York: Dutton.

Berger, M. (1995). *Germs make me sick!* (M. Hafner, Illus.). New York: HarperCollins.

Bishop, N. (2007). *Nic Bishop spiders.* New York: Scholastic.

Brown, C. L. (2007). *Beyond the dinosaurs: Monsters of the air and sea.* New York: HarperCollins.

Brown, D. (2004). *Odd boy out.* New York: Houghton Mifflin.

Burleigh, R. (2003). *Amelia Earhart: Free in the skies (American heroes).* New York: Sandpiper.

Burns, M. (2008). *The greedy triangle.* New York: Scholastic.

Cowley, J. (1999). *Red-eyed tree frog* (N. Bishop, Photo.). New York: Scholastic.

D'Aulaire, I., & D'Aulaire, E. (2008). *Abraham Lincoln.* New York: Beautiful Feet.

Davies, N. (2008). *Surprising sharks.* New York: Candlewick.

Dorros, A. (1987). *Ant cities.* New York: Crowell.

Dorros, A. (1997). *A tree is growing.* New York: Scholastic Press.

Drew, D. (1990). *The big book of animal records.* Crystal Lake, IL: Rigby.

Earle, A. (2009). *Zipping, zapping, zooming bats.* New York: Collins.

Ehlert, L. (1991). *Growing vegetable soup.* San Diego, CA: Harcourt Brace Jovanovich.

Ekoomiak, N. (1992). *Arctic memories.* New York: Holt.

Floca, B. (2009). *Moonshot: The flight of Apollo 11.* New York: Atheneum.

Garland, S. (2004). *Voices of the Alamo.* New York: Pelican.

Gibbons, G. (1997). *Nature's green umbrella: Tropical rain forests.* New York: Morrow Junior Books.

Gibbons, G. (2000). *Bats.* New York: Holiday House.

Golenbock, P. (1992). *Teammates*. San Diego, CA: Harcourt Brace Jovanovich.

Hatkoff, I., Hatkoff, C. & Kuhumbu, P. (2006). *Owen & Mzee: The true story of a remarkable friendship*. New York: Scholastic.

Jenkins, S. (1998). *Hottest, coldest, highest, deepest*. Boston: Houghton Mifflin.

Knowlton, J. (1997). *Geography from a to z: A picture glossary*. New York: HarperCollins.

Krull, K. (2008). *Hilary Rodham Clinton: Dreams taking flight*. New York: Simon & Schuster.

Markle, S. (2004). *Great white sharks*. New York: Carolrhoda.

Martin, B., & Sampson, M. (2003). *I pledge allegiance*. Boston: Candlewick Press.

Martin, J. (2009). *Snowflake Bentley*. Boston: Houghton Mifflin.

Posada, M. (2002). *Ladybugs: Red, fiery and bright*. New York: Carolrhoda.

Rappaport, D. (2001). *Martin's big words: The life of Dr. Martin Luther King, Jr.* New York: Hyperion.

Rappaport, D. (2007). *Abe's honest words: The life of Abraham Lincoln*. New York: Hyperion.

Saunders-Smith, G. (1998). *Koalas*. Mankato, MN: Capstone.

Saunders-Smith, G. (2000). *Butterflies*. Mankato, MN: Capstone.

Selsam, M. (1992). *How kittens grow*. New York: Scholastic.

Smith, R. (1999). *Sea otter rescue: The aftermath of an oil spill*. New York: Puffin.

Stewart, J., & Salem, L. (2003). *Toad or frog?* New York: Continental Press.

Waters, K. (2008). *Sarah Morton's day: A day in the life of a pilgrim girl*. New York: Scholastic.

Intermediate Books (Grades 4–6)

Ancona, G. (1992). *Man and mustang*. New York: Simon & Schuster.

Arnold, C. (1993). *On the brink of extinction: The California condor*. New York: Harcourt Brace Jovanovich. (also M).

Ball, J. (2005). *Go figure! A totally cool book about numbers*. New York: DK Children.

Berger, M. (1996). *A whale is not a fish and other animal mix-ups*. New York: Scholastic.

Burleigh, R. (1997). *Flight: The journey of Charles Lindbergh*. Logan, IA: Perfection Learning.

Charles, O. (1990). *How is a crayon made?* New York: Aladdin.

Cherry, L. (2002). *A river ran wild: An environmental history*. Queensland, Australia: Sandpiper.

Clements, G. (2009). *The picture history of great explorers*. New York: Frances Lincoln.

Deem, J. (2006). *Bodies from the ash: Life and death in ancient Pompeii*. New York: Houghton Mifflin.

Fowler, A. (1997). *Gator or croc?* Danbury, CT: Children's Press.

Freedman, R. (1995). *Immigrant kids*. New York: Puffin.

Fritz, J. (1996). *Why don't you get a horse, Sam Adams?* New York: Putnam Juvenile.

George, J. C. (2000). *How to talk to your dog*. New York: HarperCollins.

Gibbons, G. (1990). *Sunken treasure*. New York: HarperCollins.

Greenberg, J. (2008). *Christo and Jeanne-Claude: Through the gates and beyond*. New York: Roaring Brook Press.

Hollander, P., & Hollander, Z. (1996). *Amazing but true sports stories*. New York: Scholastic.

Hoyt-Goldsmith, D. (1995). *Day of the dead: A Mexican-American celebration*. New York: Holiday.

Hoyt-Goldsmith, D. (2001). *Celebrating Ramadan*. New York: Holiday House.

Iggulden, C., & Iggulden, H. (2007). *The dangerous book for boys*. New York: Collins.

Jeffrey, L. S. (2004). *Dogs: How to choose and care for a dog*. New York: Enslow.

Jenkins, S., & Page, R. (2003). *What do you do with a tail like this?* Boston: Houghton Mifflin.

Kalman, B. (2004). *The life cycle of an earthworm*. New York: Crabtree.

Keenan, S. (2007). *Animals in the house: A history of pets and people*. New York: Scholastic.

Knight, M. B. (1995). *Talking walls*. Gardiner, ME: Tilbury House.

Krull, K. (2009). *Giants of science: Marie Curie*. New York: Puffin.

Levine, E. (1993). *If you traveled on the underground railroad*. New York: Scholastic.

Lindbergh, R. (1996). *A view from the air: Charles Lindbergh's earth and sky*. New York: Puffin.

Llewellyn, C. (2005). *Crafts and games around the world*. New York: Pearson.

Markle, S. (1991). *Outside and inside you*. New York: Bradbury Press.

Micucci, C. (1997). *The life and times of the honeybee*. New York: Houghton Mifflin.

National Geographic Society. (1997). *Restless earth*. Washington, DC: National Geographic.

Parsons, A. (1993). *Eyewitness juniors amazing snakes*. New York: Dorling Kindersley. (also P).

Patent, D. H. (2003). *Slinky, scaly, slithery snakes* New York: Walker.

Reeder, T. (2005). *Poison dart frogs*. Washington, DC: National Geographic.

Reeder, T. (2005). *Giant pandas*. Washington, DC: National Geographic.

Reeve, N. (1993). *Into the mummy's tomb*. New York: Scholastic/Madison Press. (also M).

Ride, S., & Okie, S. (1995). *To space and back*. New York: Lothrop, Lee & Shepard.

Rife, D. (2009). *Letters for freedom: The American Revolution*. New York: Kids Innovative.

Ryan, P. M. (2002). *When Marian sang: The true recital of Marian Anderson*. New York: Scholastic.

Schanzer, R. (2007). *George vs. George: The American revolution as seen from both sides*. Washington, DC: National Geographic.

Schlitz, L. A. (2007). *Good masters! Sweet ladies! Voices from a medieval village*. New York: Candlewick.

Scott, E. (2007). *When is a planet not a planet?: The story of Pluto*. New York: Clarion.

Sill, C. P. (2003). *About reptiles: A guide for children*. New York: Peachtree.

Simon, S. (1993). *New questions and answers about dinosaurs*. New York: HarperCollins.

Sinclair, J. (2005). *Iopeners: All about the body*. New York:Pearson.

Tanaka, S. (2010). *The buried city of Pompeii*. New York: Black Walnut/Madison Press. (also M).

Tanaka, S. (2010). *Graveyard of the dinosaurs*. New York: Black Walnut/Madison Press. (also M).

Tanaka, S. (2010). *On board the Titanic: What it was like when the great liner sank*. New York: Black Walnut/Madison Press.

Twist, C. (2007). *The book of stars*. New York: Scholastic.

Walsh, K. (n.d.). *Time for Kids: Our world*. New York: Time for Kids.

Winters, K. (2008). *Colonial voices: Hear them speak*. New York: Dutton.

Middle-Level Books (Grades 7–9)

Atkin, S. B. (2000). *Voices from the fields: Children of migrant workers tell their stories*. New York: Little Brown. (also YA).

Bartoletti, S. C. (1999). *Growing up in coal country*. New York: Houghton Mifflin.

Bash, B. (2002). *Desert giant: The world of the saguaro cactus*. San Francisco: Sierra Club Books for Children.

Beil, K. M. (1999). *Fire in their eyes: Wildfires and the people who fight them*. San Diego, CA: Harcourt Brace.

Blumberg, R. (1989). *The great American gold rush*. New York: Atheneum.

Cone, M. (1995). *Come back, salmon: How a group of dedicated kids adopted Pigeon Creek and brought it back to life*. San Francisco: Sierra Club Books for Children.

Deem, J. M. (2005). *Bodies from the ash*. New York: Houghton Mifflin.

Freedman, R. (1989). *Lincoln: A photobiography*. New York: Clarion Books.

Freedman, R. (2002). *Confucius: The golden rule*. New York: Arthur Levine Books.

Freedman, R. (2002). *Give me liberty!: The story of the Declaration of Independence*. New York: Holiday House. (also YA).

Freedman, R. (1998). *Kids at work: Lewis Hine and the crusade against child labor*. New York: Clarion Books.

Getz, D. (1996). *Frozen man*. New York: Holt.

Hopkinson, D. (2004). *Shutting out the sky: Life in the tenements of New York, 1880–1924*. New York: Orchard Books.

Jiang, J. L. (2008). *Red scarf girl: A memoir of the cultural revolution*. New York: HarperCollins.

Krull, K. (1995). *Lives of the artists: Masterpieces, messes (and what the neighbors thought)*. San Diego, CA: Harcourt Brace. (also YA).

Krull, K. (1997). *Lives of the athletes: Thrills, spills (and what the neighbors thought)*. San Diego, CA: Harcourt Brace. (also YA).

Krull, K. (2000). *Lives of extraordinary women: Rulers, rebels (and what the neighbors thought)*. San Diego, CA: Harcourt Brace. (also YA).

Krull, K. (2002). *Lives of the musicians: Good times, bad times (and what the neighbors thought)*. San Diego, CA: Sandpiper. (also YA).

Lauber, P. (1992). *Tales mummies tell*. New York: Scholastic.

Lauber, P. (1996). *Flood: Wrestling with the Mississippi*. Washington, DC: National Geographic.

Lauber, P. (2001). *Hurricanes: Earth's mightiest storms*. New York: Houghton MifflinPress. (also I).

Levine, E. (1995). *A fence away from freedom*. New York: Putnam Juvenile.

Macaulay, D. (2008). *The way we work*. Boston: Houghton Mifflin.

Mannis, C. D. (2003). *The queen's progress: An Elizabethan alphabet.* New York: Viking.

McKissack, P., & McKissack, F. L. (1999). *Christmas in the big house, Christmas in the quarters.* New York: Scholastic.

Montgomery, S. (2004). *The man-eating tigers of Sundarbans.* Boston: Houghton Mifflin.

Nelson, K. (2008). *We are the ship: The story of Negro league baseball.* New York: Hyperion.

Pringle, L. (2001). *Global warming.* New York: Seastar.

Reeves, N. (1993). *Into the mummy's tomb.* New York: Scholastic/Madison Press.

Ride, S., & O'Shaughnessy, T. (2009). *Mission: Planet earth: Our world and its climate—and how humans are changing them.* New York: FlashPoint. (also YA).

Rol, R., & Verhoeven, R. (1995). *Anne Frank, beyond the diary: A photographic remembrance.* New York: Viking.

Sattler, H. R. (1995). *Our patchwork planet: The story of plate tectonics.* New York: Lothrop, Lee & Shepard.

Schlitz, L. (2008). *Good masters! Sweet ladies!* New York: Candlewick.

Scott, E. (1998). *Close encounters: Exploring the universe with the Hubble space telescope.* New York: Hyperion Books for Children. (also YA).

Scott, E. (2007). *When is a planet not a planet? The story of Pluto.* New York: Clarion.

Stanley, J. (1993). *Children of the dust bowl: The true story of the school at Weedpatch Camp.* New York: Crown Books for Young Readers.

Stanley, J. (1998). *I am an American: A true story of the Japanese internment.* New York: Scholastic.

Tanaka, S. (2005). *Mummies: The newest, coolest & creepiest from around the world.* New York: Abrams Books.

Thimmesh, C. (2002). *Girls think of everything: Stories of ingenious inventions by women.* Boston: Houghton Mifflin.

Thimmesh, C. (2006). *Team moon: How 400,000 people landed Apollo 11 on the moon.* New York: Houghton Mifflin.

Van der Rol, R., & Verhoeven, R. (1993). *Anne Frank: Beyond the diary: A photographic remembrance.* New York: Viking.

Young Adult Books (High School)

Aliki. (2000). *William Shakespeare and The Globe.* New York: HarperCollins. (also M).

Aronson, M. (2000). *Sir Walter Ralegh and the quest for El Dorado.* New York: Clarion Books.

Bartoletti, S. C. (2001). *Black potatoes: The story of the great Irish famine, 1845–1850.* Boston: Houghton Mifflin.

Beah, I. (2007). *A long way gone: Memoirs of a boy soldier.* New York: Farrar, Straus & Giroux.

Blumenthal, K. (2005). *Let me play!: The story of Title IX: The law that changed the future of girls in America.* New York: Atheneum.

Bodanis, D. (2001). *E = mc² : A biography of the world's most famous equation.* New York: Berkley Trade.

D'Aluisio, F. (2008). *What the world eats.* New York: Tricycle Press.

Dash, J. (2000). *The longitude prize.* New York: Frances Foster Books. (also M).

Farrell, J. (1998). *Invisible enemies: Stories of infectious disease.* New York: Farrar, Straus & Giroux.

Farrell, J. (2005). *Invisible allies: Microbes that shape our lives.* New York: Farrar, Straus and Giroux.

Fleischman, J. (2004). *Phineas Gage: A gruesome but true story about brain science.* New York: Houghton Mifflin.

Frank, M. (2005). *Understanding the Holy Land: Answering questions about the Israeli–Palestinean conflict.* New York: Viking.

Green, D. (2008). *Biology: Life as we know it.* New York: Kingfisher.

Hoose, P. (2001). *We were there too!* New York: Farrar, Straus & Giroux.

Jenkins, S. (2002). *Life on earth: The story of evolution.* New York: Houghton Mifflin.

Johnson, G. (2009). *Animal tracks and signs.* Washington, DC: National Geographic.

King, C., & Osborne, L. B. (1997). *Oh freedom!: Kids talk about the Civil Rights movement with the people who made it happen.* New York: Knopf.

Lobel, A. (2008). *No pretty pictures: A child of war*. New York: HarperCollins.

McPherson, J. (2002). *Fields of fury: The American Civil War*. New York: Atheneum.

McWhorter, D. (2005). *A dream of freedom: The Civil Rights movement from 1954–1958*. New York: Scholastic.

Myers, W. D. (2001). *The greatest Muhammed Ali*. New York: Scholastic.

Partridge, E. (2002). *This land was made for you and me: The life and songs of Woody Guthrie*. New York: Viking.

Partridge, E. (2005). *John Lennon: All I want is the truth*. New York: Viking.

Sherrow, V. (1996). *Violence and the media: The question of cause and effect*. New York: Millbrook Press.

Siegel, S. C. (2006). *To dance: A ballerina's graphic novel*. New York: Atheneum/Richard Jackson.

Stone, T. L. (2009). *Almost astronauts: 13 women who dared to dream*. New York: Candlewick.

Thomson, S., Mortenson, G., & Relin, D. O. (2009). *Three cups of tea: One man's journey to change the world … One child at a time*. New York: Puffin.

Warren, A. (2001). *Surviving Hitler: A boy in the Nazi death camps*. New York: HarperCollins.

Welden, A. (2001). *Girls who rocked the world: Heroines from Sacajawea to Sheryl Swoopes*. Hillsboro, OR: Beyond Words. (also M).

Quality Informational Magazines

Ask

Cobblestone

Kids Discover

Know

National Geographic Kids

Odyssey

Ranger Rick

Sports Illustrated Kids

Time for Kids

Yes Mag

Zoobooks

Faces

Quality Informational Websites

All About Explorers
www.allaboutexplorers.com/explorers

California Department of Education Recommended Literature for Mathematics and Science
www.cde.ca.gov/ci/sc/ll

California Department of Education Recommended Readings in Literature K–12
www.cde.ca.gov/ci/sc/ll/index/ap/litsearch.asp

Discovery Channel School
school.discoveryeducation.com

Library of Congress Teacher Resources
www.loc.gov/teachers

National Council for the Social Studies Notable Trade Books for Young People
www.ncss.org/resources/notable

National Science Teachers Association Outstanding Science Trade Books for Students K–12
www.nsta.org/bs04

PBS Kids
pbskids.org

Vicki Cobb's Science Page
www.vickicobb.com

Virtual Manipulatives
nlvm.usu.edu/en/nav/vlibrary.html

Index